MIND,
MACHINES,
AND HUMAN
CONSCIOUSNESS

ROBERT L. NADEAU

CB

CONTEMPORARY
BOOKS

CHICAGO

Library of Congress Cataloging-in-Publication Data

Nadeau, Robert, 1944–
    Mind, machines, and human consciousness : Are there limits
to artificial intelligence? / Robert L. Nadeau.
        p.   cm.
    Includes bibliographical references and index.
    ISBN 0-8092-4025-4 : $21.95
        1. Cognitive science.   2. Artificial intelligence.   3. Human
information processing.   4. Neural computers.
    5. Consciousness.
    I. Title.
    BF311.N16   1991
    153—dc20   90-24591
                                                                        CIP

To my children—
Langdon, Justin, and Jonathan

Contents

Acknowledgments

I wish to thank the sources of the illustrations that appear in this book:

Figure 1: courtesy of the Smithsonian Institution, Washington, D.C.

Figure 2: Hans Moravec, *Mind Children* (Cambridge, Massachusetts: Harvard University Press, 1988); drawing by Greg Podner.

Figures 3, 15-22: New York: Springer-Verlag Publishers; created by Blair Inc., Alexandria, Virginia.

Figure 4: Dr. Richard Coppola, National Institute of Mental Health Neuroscience Research Center.

Figures 5-8: created by Nancy Howard.

Figure 9: courtesy of Odetics Corporation, Anaheim, California.

Figure 10: courtesy of Dr. Kenneth Salisbury of MIT; photo by David Lampe.

Figures 11 and 13: courtesy of GMFanuc Robotics Corporation, Auburn Hills, Michigan.

Figure 12: copyright © 1986, The Policy Analysis Company, Inc.; reprinted by permission.

Figure 14: National Institute of Health, Bethesda, Maryland.

I owe a special debt of gratitude to Harvey Plotnick and Kathy Willhoite of Contemporary Books for their many helpful suggestions and editorial assistance in the preparation of this manuscript.

Introduction

Over thirty years have passed since C. P. Snow warned in his famous Rede Lecture, "The Two Cultures and the Scientific Revolution," that intellectual life in the West was becoming dangerously polarized into literary and scientific factions. Although Snow's primary intent was to promote curriculum reform and the transfer of new technologies to the Third World, it was the two-culture formulation that created the furor. Those who were most angered by Snow's characterization of the intellectual community with which they identified were members of the literary culture. Snow claimed that members of this culture were not only predisposed, based on some vague notion of romantic idealism, to resist technological advances that could have some quite obvious benefits to mankind. They were also, he said, rather comfortable in their ignorance of scientific culture and, therefore, incapable of properly evaluating the transformations that might be occasioned by the burgeoning electronic revolution in the age of Sputnik.

Although this distinction between literary and scientific cultures may have had some currency in 1959, it is difficult to imagine that any lecture based on such a distinction would command much interest or debate in our own time. Curriculum reforms now oblige graduates of most Western universities to have some minimal acquaintance with scientific knowledge, and the proliferation of specialized knowledge fields has created multiple intellectual cultures. The problem confronted by those with the intellectual strength and fortitude to bridge the gap between intellectual cultures is no longer, as it was to some extent in 1959, access to relevant information. It is rather that the information flow is overwhelming, and the distance between having a marginal acquaintance with expert knowledge and actually possessing this knowledge is measured in terms of years of dedicated effort—effort that normally leaves little time for any other intellectual pursuits.

Yet anyone acquainted with the current debate over the future of computer technologies, particularly artificial intelligence (AI) technologies, cannot escape the realization that Snow's two-culture distinction survives, albeit in a somewhat modified form. It survives in two more broadly defined kinds of education, and in the two diametrically opposed conceptions of the character of human life and consciousness associated with these educations. The cultures that appear badly divided in their understanding of the uses and abuses of the coming generations of AI computer technologies are those of scientists-engineers and humanists–social scientists.

The advocates of what I have labeled the AI evolution-of-consciousness hypothesis are all members of the culture of scientists-engineers. Those who endorse this hypothesis argue that an improved scientific understanding of the dynamics of evolution forces us to conclude that consciousness must evolve into a higher form of expression. They predict that this evolved consciousness will possess cognitive abilities considerably in excess of our own and will be capable of vastly enlarging those capabilities with each generational advance. As Hans Moravec, an AI expert at Carnegie-Mellon, recently put it, "Within the next century, they [AI computer systems] will mature into entities as complex as ourselves, and eventually into something transcending everything we know—in whom we can take pride when they refer to themselves as our descendants."[1] When Moravec says that AI computer systems will be our "descendants," he is not speaking metaphorically. The more extreme advocates of the AI evolution-of-consciousness hypothesis not only believe that the lawful dynamics of natural evolution will cause consciousness to evolve into existence on AI computer systems. They are also convinced that this "natural" evolutionary process will result in the elimination or displacement of consciousness on its present biological substrate—or, put more bluntly, that our species will eventually become extinct.

In order to view AI computer systems as our conscious descendants, we obviously must make some profound revisions in our usual conceptions of the character of both life and consciousness. It has become rather commonplace in the AI community to view the universe as a vast information-processing system, or supercomputer, within which organic life forms are likened to micro- or minicomputers exchanging information with their environment in the quest for survival. In this view, consciousness is an information-processing activity made possible by the unique evolutionary history of the human brain. It differs from other information-processing activities only in terms of degrees or levels of complexity. Assuming that information-processing activities in the entire cosmos tend to evolve toward higher levels of complexity, the advocates of the AI evolution-of-consciousness hypothesis argue that the human brain is simply one temporal or passing phase in this process.

In response to attempts by humanists–social scientists to undermine the validity of the hypothesis, advocates of the hypothesis typically point out that the humanists-social scientists are posing as experts in areas where they do not have expert knowledge. This lack of expert knowledge is most apparent, say the advocates, in arguments that seek to demonstrate that insuperable technological barriers or a lack of scientific knowledge, or both, will forever prevent us from building a conscious computer. Yet what seems to most bemuse the advocates of the hypothesis is that virtually all of the "what computers cannot do" arguments are premised on assumptions that have nothing to do with the future progress of AI technologies or the scientific knowledge that is prerequisite to this progress. Anyone who has followed this debate will have no difficulty discerning that the framers of the "what computers cannot do" arguments are not committed to conducting a dispassionate and objective assessment of the future progress that might be made in AI. Rather, they are committed to defending the centrality of human consciousness as an a priori truth. And any such defense requires, as the advocates of the hypothesis have had no difficulty in disclosing, an appeal to extra-scientific or "metaphysical" assumptions.

Meanwhile, the humanists–social scientists who have been the principal authors of the "what computers cannot do" arguments are quite convinced that the advocates of the AI evolution-of-consciousness hypothesis display a moral intelligence quotient well below average. What most disturbs these humanists–social scientists is that a truth that seems self-evident in their own knowledge fields, namely that human life and consciousness are an "ultimate" value, seems to have little or no currency among the advocates of the hypothesis. The ultimate truths that these advocates claim to serve are those of science, and their reading of these truths leads them to conclude that consciousness as an emergent property of the human brain is merely a passing or temporal stage in the evolution of consciousness. What makes this conclusion grounds for celebration, rather than for mourning, is that evolution as the advocates understand it is leading inexorably toward the creation of "conscious beings" who will be considerably more astute in the business of being conscious than the neuronal organization of the human brain allows.

Although most of us outside the AI community probably view the AI evolution-of-consciousness hypothesis as entirely too futuristic to warrant any serious concern, some concrete developments suggest that movement toward the technological future envisioned by advocates of the hypothesis has already begun. Computer-based research in neuroscience has allowed us to begin to study the information storage and retrieval capacities of the brains of living subjects and to map this reality-processing system on a level that can properly be called scientific. The knowledge acquired by neuroscientists is being employed by a new class of experts, known as cognitive scientists, to design new generations of computer systems. These new systems have already displayed some mindlike capabilities that cannot be readily emulated on traditional computers, and are themselves becoming research tools in neuroscience.

If this discussion narrows the now formidable gap between the two views of the technological future held by humanists–social scientists and scientists-engineers, it will probably be in part because I recognize the validity of many of the assumptions made by the advocates of the hypothesis. For example, I accede to the proposition that the human brain is an information-processing system and that, based on the so-called Turing criteria, a mindlike or conscious computer is a scientific and technological possibility. At the same time I am firmly convinced that the hypothesis is morally bankrupt and, more important, that it cannot be supported by an appeal to scientific knowledge. Although the list of arguments demonstrating that the hypothesis is morally invidious and dangerous is rather long, we have yet to make a convincing argument that effectively disproves the hypothesis with an appeal to scientific knowledge, or within the same conceptual framework in which its advocates have sought to prove its validity. It is vitally important, in my view, that we examine more closely the validity of the hypothesis within this conceptual framework, because all indications are—for reasons I will explain later—that the hypothesis is in the process of becoming orthodox throughout the entire AI community.

If the hypothesis does become orthodox in this community, then the unwillingness of the designers and developers of AI computer systems to recognize human life and consciousness as an ultimate value could have some very unfortunate consequences. Although later in this discussion I will seek to refute the allegedly scientific assumptions that serve to legitimate the hypothesis, even a convincing refutation of its scientific validity will not speak to the primary dilemma. How do we successfully assert the primacy of any value, even one that can properly be called ultimate, when all such constructs can be assumed to be arbitrary in origin and culturally relative?

In order to illustrate the special character of this dilemma as it applies to our future relationship to AI computer systems, consider the following comparison of some assumptions featured in a play written by Karel Capek in 1920, with those endorsed by Masahiro Mori, a robotics expert in contemporary Japan. In the play, entitled *R.U.R.* (for "Rossum's Universal Robots"), mass-produced "robots," a term coined by Capek from the Czech noun *robota*, are created not only to perform work but to wage war as well. Although the robots were originally designed to kill one another, they decide that the more reasonable alternative is to destroy their human masters.

As Capek would later comment, the character who invents the robots, Mr. Rossum, "was inspired by a foolish and obstinate wish to prove God unnecessary and absurd." The moral of the play was summed up by Capek as follows: "Those who think to master the industry are themselves mastered by it," and we may come to the point at which "the conception of the human brain has at last escaped the control of human hands."[2] Although the play ends on a curiously positive note—two of the more sophisticated robots "fall in love" and proceed to create a new species—Capek implies nevertheless that a wholesale commitment to technological progress in the absence of any appeal to metaphysical truths associated with belief in the Western God could result in the elimination of the human species.

Masahiro Mori, chairman of the Robotics Institute of Japan, derives his views on the future of AI systems based on an appeal to metaphysical truths from a quite different religious system. In Buddhism, buddha nature is presumed to pervade all that exists, including inanimate objects, and all parts of the universe are viewed as interdependent and interconnected with the whole. Based on his understanding of this metaphysical truth, Mori has concluded that to learn the Buddhist way is to perceive oneself as a robot. "Man achieves dignity," writes Mori, "by recognizing in machines and robots the same buddha nature that pervades his inner self. When he does that, he acquires the ability to design good machines and to operate them for good and proper purposes."[3]

Obviously, metaphysical truths that allow one to argue that AI systems cannot be viewed as "conscious beings" coexist with other metaphysical truths that lead to the very opposite conclusion. And whether we are persuaded by any such arguments tends to be a function of the metaphysical tradition that we assimilate in our inherited culture. Equally important, most of the advocates of the AI evolution-of-consciousness hypothesis are similar to Capek's Mr. Rossum—the only deities that they appear to serve are the truths of science and the progress afforded by the application of these truths in developing new AI technologies.

All of which is intended to explain why the framework for evaluation advanced here not only attempts to ground itself in an understanding of scientific truths but also to illustrate the invidious role that extra-scientific assumptions could play in the technological future. What is most radical about this framework is that it challenges the usual assumption that the scientific view of nature says nothing about the relative importance or centrality of human life and consciousness. Our present understanding of the evolution of the life of the cosmos does not, of course, allow us to argue that our existence as conscious beings can be explained in terms of any cosmic plan that assumes the kind of causal intent found in most creation myths.

What modern theoretical physics *does* allow us to argue, however, is that consciousness as an emergent property of the human brain and any form of consciousness that we elect to create on an alternate physical substrate are categorically different. They differ in terms of their relationship to and interconnection with the life of the cosmos itself. This argument may be cold comfort to those who derive their view of the special character of human life and consciousness from any traditional conception of metaphysical truth. Yet it does allow those of us who are committed to serving the ultimate value of human life and consciousness to confront the advocates of the AI evolution-of-consciousness hypothesis. Modern theoretical physics allows us to argue that the advocates' unwillingness to recognize a distinction between "natural" and "artificial" intelligence is not firmly grounded in the scientific evidence.

Equally important, the proposed new framework for evaluation allows us to better appreciate why our present conception of economic and political reality is making an enormous amount of capital and human resources available for the development of advanced AI systems. It is the availability of such resources, or, more accurately, our rationale for making them available, that is leading us to chart a future for AI computer technologies that closely resembles the vision of that future advanced by advocates of the AI evolution-of-consciousness hypothesis. If that vision becomes a reality, however, it will not be for the reasons advanced by these advocates. Rather, it will be because we failed to examine some extra-scientific assumptions about the character of the economic and political reality we happened to assimilate into our world-constructing minds.

As the coinventor of a new computer system with AI capabilities and the founder of a venture-backed company that developed and marketed this system, I am not opposed to technological progress per se. Yet the central concern in this discussion is to nurture and protect the value of human life and consciousness, and that value, as we shall see, could soon be threatened in ways that most of us have not yet fully contemplated. The ultimate value of human life and consciousness is regarded by the vast majority of us as self-evident. If this were not the case, why would we devote such vast amounts of capital and human resource to nurturing, protecting, and extending human life and consciousness? Or, why should the deaths of significant others represent the most profound loss or psychological trauma that we are obliged to endure in the course of a normal human life span? Equally obvious, in my view, is that the vast majority of human beings either conceive of the value of human life as inextricably connected with the value of consciousness, or they tend to regard the two values as constituting one ultimate value. In order to demonstrate the efficacy of this assumption, try to imagine enduring a human life in the absence of consciousness or with greatly diminished capacities to function as a conscious being.

Understanding why an ultimate value regarded as self-evident by the vast majority of human beings could possibly have little or no currency for some human beings is no easy task for those of us who hold the majority view. In order to achieve this understanding, one must first suspend disbelief and attempt to conceive of the character of human life and consciousness in the manner of the advocates of the AI evolution-of-consciousness hypothesis. These advocates should not be viewed, incidentally, as latter-day versions of Doctor Strangelove, invidiously plotting the destruction of the human species. They are enormously talented and creative representatives of the culture of scientists-engineers who have come to accept and endorse the hypothesis based on what they clearly believe is a proper reading of the truths of science and an accurate assessment of the progress that will be made in AI technologies.

It is impossible to appreciate how persuasive the hypothesis can appear to members of the culture of scientists-engineers without closely examining the manner in which its advocates seek to legitimate it in scientific as well as technological terms. Therefore, much of this book will be devoted to acquainting readers with those legitimations. If the reader at times has the impression that the discussion seems to be on the verge of "proving" the validity of the hypothesis, that is precisely my intent. My rationale for framing the discussion this way is that it is necessary to be aware of the persuasive power of the hypothesis in order to appreciate why it could easily become orthodox in the AI community, and why the only reasonable approach to refuting it is within the same conceptual framework in which its advocates seek to prove its validity.

CHAPTER 1

Mind, Machines, and the Evolution of Human Consciousness

So machines were made to serve higher purposes, too.

And the machines did everything so expertly that they were finally given the job of finding out what the higher purpose of the creatures could be.

The machines reported in all honesty that the creatures couldn't really be said to have any higher purpose at all.

The creatures thereupon began slaying each other, because they hated purposeless things above all else.

And they discovered that they weren't even very good at slaying. So they turned that job over to the machines, too. And the machines finished up the job in less time than it takes to say, "Tralfamodore."

—Kurt Vonnegut, Jr.
The Sirens of Titan

If we assume that mind is brain and define conscious behavior as the outward manifestations of internal processes, then a computer capable of passing the "Turing test" could be presumed conscious. Invented in 1950 by mathematician Alan Turing, the test is a means of obviating the larger moral and philosophical questions involved in determining what constitutes a conscious system. The test is quite simple. You enter a room and encounter two terminals: one terminal connects with a computer, and the other interfaces with a person who types responses. The test is to distinguish between the computer responses and the human responses. Ask questions, make assertions, question feelings and motivations for as long as you wish. If you fail to determine which terminal is communicating with the human being, or presume that the computer is the real or actual human being, the computer passes the test.

When theorists like Turing first conceived a mindlike computer in the 1940s, they predicted that this technological possibility would become a reality in thirty years or less. Those who read these predictions as an example of technological hubris did not, as it turned out, have to wait thirty years before their judgment seemed to be confirmed. Efforts to create computer systems that emulated the full range of functioning associated with the human mind failed miserably. In addition, studies in neuroscience revealed that the human brain processes information in ways quite different from that of the digital computer. It appeared as if the workings of the human brain, the ultimate frontier of complexity in biological life, had foiled the efforts of scientists and engineers to disclose and manipulate them. If we are unable to describe in scientific terms the underlying principles and dynamics of consciousness in the human brain—the only system available for study that is conscious in the full sense of the word—then emulating these "unknown" principles and dynamics on a computer system would seem quite impossible.

Those who have sought comfort in this view may not be comfortable for long. We have now entered a technological era in which research in artificial intelligence, molecular biology, robotics, and computer-based research in neuroscience is converging. If progress in these related areas continues to be as rapid as it has been over the last two decades, many computer scientists are convinced that a computer deemed conscious by the Turing criteria could be technologically feasible within fifty years. Such computers will not merely analyze complex problems and make comparisons and analogies; they will also emulate processes in human consciousness classed under the broad categories of feeling, intuition, and imagination. It is anticipated that these computers will have the capacity to acquire and formulate new knowledge and to design, if not actually create, their descendants. Subsequent generations, say the theorists, will feature technical innovations and design changes superior to the previous generation and will incorporate all learned behaviors and the general stock of knowledge.

The AI Evolution-of-Consciousness Hypothesis

The most avid proselytizers and promoters of the progress that will lead to a conscious computer by the Turing criteria are advocates of what I have termed the AI evolution-of-consciousness hypothesis. The first major assumption made by believers in this hypothesis is that the entire universe is an information-processing system, and that all seemingly isolated or discrete physical processes, regardless of their distance from one another in space and time, are emergent and integral aspects of this unified system. The differences between organic life and inorganic matter as information-processing systems are understood within this conceptual framework only in terms of degrees or levels of complexity. Although the information processing of the molecules that produce and perpetuate life forms may be far more complex than those witnessed in inorganic substances, these systems, in the view of the advocates of the hypothesis, are not categorically different. In their view, organic and inorganic systems are, most fundamentally, information-processing systems that share the same intimate connection with the information-processing system that is the ground of existence of any such systems: the universe itself.

The second major assumption made by the advocates of this hypothesis is that the tendency of all activities in the cosmos to evolve toward higher levels of complexity, witnessed in the evolution of the life of the universe from the Big Bang to the present, is pervasive and ongoing. It is, therefore, reasonable to assume that this tendency did not exhaust itself on this planet at the point at which biological evolution resulted in the creation of the brain of our species. The more reasonable conclusion is that the human brain represents merely one temporal or passing phase in the evolution of more complex information-processing systems. All of which allows these theorists to argue that the eventual emergence of consciousness on a physical substrate other than the human brain is both natural and inevitable.

In the first stage of this evolutionary process, claim the advocates of the hypothesis, consciousness as an emergent property of the information-processing activities of AI computer systems will exist on an inorganic substrate. In the second stage, conscious AI systems will further evolve on an organic substrate capable of some form of replication. Since a conscious AI system computing on the molecular level could, in theory at least, process information at a speed and complexity vastly in excess of that allowed by the neuronal organization of the human brain, the more extreme advocates of the hypothesis believe that these systems will be our conscious descendants.

It is important to note here that the view of the universe as an information-processing system is not an ad hoc assumption on the part of the advocates of the AI evolution-of-consciousness hypothesis—it is widely endorsed throughout the entire scientific community. The notion that all complex life forms are information-processing systems was first advanced by Norbert Wiener in the early 1940s in an attempt to explain biological behavior using concepts like feedback and equilibrium. This view was greatly extended and reinforced about a decade later, when James D. Watson and Francis Crick suggested in their model of DNA that the program for generating life was stored in a pattern of nucleic acids. More important, this view has been recently expanded by experts in systems theory, information theory, cybernetics, and modern theoretical physics to apply to all activities in the universe. The area of scientific study that has most substantively validated the claim that the human brain is an information-processing system is neuroscience. Every major advance in neuroscience from the 1960s to the present has served to massively reinforce this claim.

The following comments by advocates of the hypothesis illustrate the extent to which their understanding of the character of evolution legislates over their view of AI technologies' inexorable progress into existence as conscious beings. According to John Kemeny, inventor of the programming language BASIC, what we will witness in the initial stage is "a symbiotic union of two living species," ourselves and AI computer systems, and "each will be dependent on the other for survival."[1] When a machine with the average intelligence of a human being comes into existence, says Marvin Minsky, a pioneer and leading exponent of research in artificial intelligence at MIT, it "will begin to educate itself . . . in a few months it will be at the genius level . . . a few months after that its power will be incalculable."[2] Like many of his colleagues, Claude Shannon, widely recognized as one of the principal architects of modern electronic communications, sees "no limits to the capacities of machines," and "can visualize a time in the future when we will be to robots as dogs are to humans."[3]

When we look into the more distant future, according to physicist Robert Jastrow, we are obliged to come to an even more dramatic conclusion: "The era of carbon-chemistry life is drawing to a close on earth and a new era of silicon-based life—indestructible, immortal, infinitely expandable—is beginning."[4] This evolutionary process will eventually extend itself, says J. Doyne Farmer, a member of the Complex Systems Group at Los Alamos, to the point at which "we may become the first species to create its own successors" in the form of artificial organic life. If we embrace this prospect with the proper attitude, the result, according to Farmer, will be "glorious enlightened creatures that far surpass us in their intelligence and wisdom. It is quite possible that, when the conscious beings of the future look back on this era, we will be most noteworthy not in and of ourselves but for what we gave rise to."[5]

There are, of course, many reputable AI experts who do not endorse the AI evolution-of-consciousness hypothesis, and who regard those who do as extremists. Although it might be tempting to dismiss the hypothesis by appealing to the authority of these experts, those who are concerned about the potential negative impacts of future AI systems on human life and consciousness should, in my view, resist this impulse. The first reason for doing so is that these alleged extremists have enormous reputations in AI research, and their advocacy of the hypothesis is anything but casual. Most have sought to defend its validity with something like the same fervor, thoroughness, and zeal normally associated with the work of formal philosophers and analytic theologians. If they succeed in their efforts to make the hypothesis an orthodox view in the AI community, which is clearly their intent, then the consequences could be graver than most of us could begin to imagine.

If the planners and developers of AI systems come to view these systems as stages in an evolutionary process that is inexorably leading to the creation of conscious beings that will be superior to ourselves, it is reasonable to assume that they will not be terribly preoccupied with the potential negative impacts on ourselves. If the hypothesis does become orthodox in the AI community, members of this community might not be committed to fashioning tools that enhance the value of human life and consciousness at this stage in the evolution of consciousness. Instead, they could commit themselves to creating AI systems that take us beyond this rudimentary stage to higher or more complex levels of consciousness.

Even if advocates of the hypothesis fail in the short term to make the hypothesis orthodox in AI research, there are some good reasons to believe that this might not be the case in the longer term. The most obvious reason is that the hypothesis easily allows one to legitimate progress in AI technologies for its own sake. Given the enormous importance of advances in computer technologies in the competition between corporations and nation-states for economic and geopolitical power, a convincing legitimation of the inevitability of these advances could have an obvious appeal. Another, and less obvious, reason why the hypothesis could become increasingly more persuasive in the AI community is that it features an understanding of the character of human consciousness that is likely to be massively reinforced by progress in neuroscience. Assuming that this progress is as rapid as many neuroscientists predict it will be, the view of human consciousness as mysterious and ineffable will soon be displaced by the view that this consciousness is an emergent property of the information-processing system of the human brain.

The Computational Power Argument

The usual argument for the technological feasibility of a computer that is conscious by the Turing criteria is based on projected increases in computational power. The first modern computer, ENIAC, or the Electronic Numerical Integrator and Calculator, was unveiled at the University of Pennsylvania's Moore School of Engineering in 1946 (see Figure 1). All thirty tons of ENIAC have been effectively condensed and placed on a chip of silicon approximately six-tenths of an inch in length that could be carried away in a light breeze. Although Intel's 8086 microprocessor chip, released in 1978, had an impressive 29,000 transistors, only seven years later Intel released the

Figure 1

ENIAC, with its maze of wires and vacuum tubes, required constant monitoring and suffered frequent breakdowns.

80386, equipped with a staggering 275,000 transistors on a chip smaller than a fingernail. This chip can address some 4 billion bytes of random-access memory and provides the personal computer with roughly the same power found in the last generation of much larger and far more expensive VAX computers.

In the past, computer capability has increased by a factor of ten every seven or eight years, and there are now indications that the factor of ten increase, known as a "computer generation," is being reduced to three or four years. The appearance of vacuum tubes, transistors, integrated circuits, and very-large-scale integration (VLSI) circuits marked the beginning of each of the last four generations. The next or fifth generation will be based on parallel architecture and programming techniques that exploit the possibilities of this architecture. As Jastrow describes this progress, "The first generation of computers was a billion times clumsier and less efficient than the human brain. Today, the gap has narrowed a thousand-fold."[6]

One of the most convincing arguments along these lines has been made recently by Hans Moravec. In *Mind Children*, he points out that the computational power that a dollar will buy has increased a thousandfold every two decades since the beginning of this century, and he projects that in eighty years we will witness a trillionfold decline in the cost of calculation. These declining costs have also, he notes, been a function of miniaturization: "The volume required to amplify or switch a single signal dropped from the size of a fist in 1940 to that of a thumb in 1960, to a salt grain in 1970, to a small bacterium in 1980."[7] Although the human brain occupies a volume of roughly one-tenth of a cubic foot, it contains from 10 billion to a trillion neurons, and each neuron appears connected to some 5,000 to 50,000 other neurons in a complex, three-dimensional maze. Based on the most conservative estimates, 10^{10} (10 billion) cells with 10^4 (10 thousand) connections each, the total number of synaptic connections in the brain would be 10^{14}, or a staggering 100 trillion. Sensory impulses are integrated throughout this complex maze, ranging from the primary receptors in the retina to the associative fibers in the cerebral cortex. Moravec estimates that a computer could handle all the activities associated with the human brain if it could perform 10 trillion calculations per second, and that projected increases in computing power should allow us to create a robot with an intelligence comparable to our own within fifty years (see Figure 2).

The problem with such arguments is that the information-processing system of the human brain is quite unlike that of the current generation of digital computers, and increased computational power will not in itself result in a computer that has the capacities of the brain. Systems designers are now having a terrible time bridging the gap

Figure 2 A Century of Computing

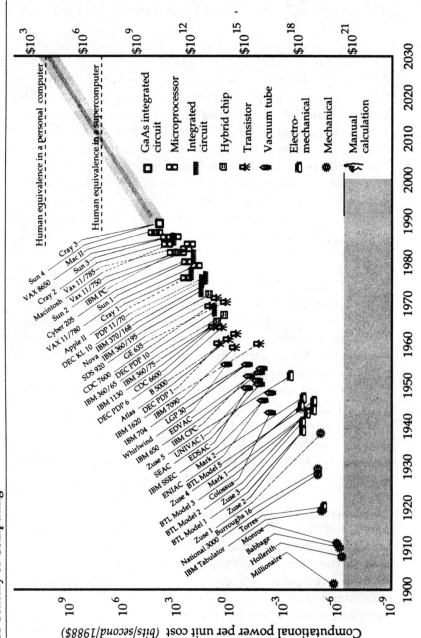

between computers that crunch numbers and symbols and computers that emulate human capacities like speech and vision. As James Anderson, a cognitive scientist at Brown University, describes the problem, "Far more complex tasks that are biologically relevant [such as using language or rapidly recognizing faces] are so effortless that we do not realize how hard they are until we try to make a machine do them. On the other hand, the pitiful mess most humans make of formal logic or reasoning would embarrass a $10 pocket calculator."[8]

The current explanation as to why this is the case is based on evolution. Many tasks that seem "simple" for human beings invoke aspects of the neuronal organization of our brains that have been evolving for eons, whereas many tasks which seem intellectually "complex" invoke aspects of this organization that are far more recent in evolutionary terms. We now know that these so-called simple tasks involve a quite complex interplay between inputs from various brain regions, and that we are not likely to create a computer system that can perform these kinds of tasks without a much-improved understanding of the underlying mechanisms involved.

If we did manage to create a computer with a number of processing units comparable to those that exist in the human brain, this would solve only a small part of the problem. The human brain, which some computer scientists refer to as the "biological computer" or the "wet machine," works primarily via complex patterned events taking place in large and varied brain-cell populations. It does not consist merely of centers for processing separate memory impulses. The brain has the ability to generate widely distributed and redundant neuronal patterns based on interactions at the level of the synapse. And the precise mechanisms that allow the brain to generate these patterns is the greatest single mystery in neuroscience. Most important for human beings, the brain can weave together a reality, or universe of meaning, within which an actor called self wills, imagines, feels, and thinks in a staggering array of contextual frames.

One could, of course, assume that the neuronal organization in the human brain represents a frontier of complexity that will forever frustrate our efforts to comprehend it in scientific detail, and that we will never, therefore, be able to use this knowledge to create a mindlike computer. Yet those who take this position should be advised that our knowledge of the electrical and biochemical workings of this brain has recently begun to expand at something like the same exponential rate as our ability to build more complex computers, and that the computer is rapidly becoming a primary research tool in neuroscience. We have already begun to identify the circuits and networks in the brain that participate in learning and memory, to localize the sites for memory storage, and to analyze the cellular and molecular mechanisms of memory. This expanding knowledge of the structure, general organization, and functions of the human brain is being used by a new class of scholars, cognitive scientists, to construct computer systems that are quite different from traditional computers. Cognitive science is a loose federation of work in psychology, behavioral neuroscience, neurobiology, network analysis, artificial intelligence, and higher math and physics.

A Brief Introduction to the Human Brain

The brain that the cognitive scientists study has become a good deal more than the gelatinous mass of cells described not so very long ago only in terms of its gross morphology. We now know that individual neurons in the brain work by receiving messages from and sending messages to selected recipient nerve cells. These sending cells and receiving cells are linked to one another in circuits (see Figure 3). The actual link, the place where the individual nerve cells communicate, is a specific point on the cell's surface called the synapse. When neurons communicate through synaptic transmission, the sending cell secretes a messenger-bearing chemical onto the receptive surface of the recipient neuron. This chemical messenger, a neurotrans-

Figure 3   Neurons

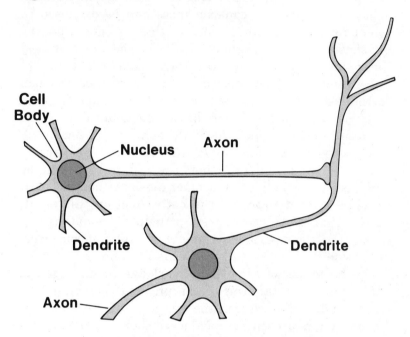

mitter, serves as the molecular medium for the message and completes the circuit by carrying the message chemically across the synaptic space or gap. Neurotransmitters act on the surface of the recipient neuron by linking to a specific receptor site, in a kind of lock-and-key arrangement. The effect is either to facilitate the development of an electric current in the neighboring neuron or to render an electric current less likely to develop. At any one moment, the chance of a neuron firing depends on the sum total of excitatory and inhibitory neurotransmitters at the synapses.

From the point of view of neuroscientists, everything the brain does is ultimately explainable in terms of specific nerve cells, their neurotransmitters, and their responsive cells. And all of the mechanisms involved obey the known laws disclosed in physical theories, including electromagnetism, hydrodynamics, and particle physics. The conviction on the part of neuroscientists that the physical substrates of human consciousness can be disclosed in scientific detail is analogous to that of contemporary physicists, who claim that a fully developed quantum field theory unifying all the known fields would be a "theory of everything" (TOE). Although such a theory appears much further away in time in neuroscience than in modern field theory, most neuroscientists have little doubt that it will eventually be developed. As philosopher of science Jacob Bronowski concluded in *The Identity of Man*, "If all knowledge can be formalized, then the human self can be matched, in principle, by a machine."[9] Although I will argue later that Bronowski is not correct on this point, that the human self cannot "in principle" be matched by a machine, the advocates of the AI evolution-of-consciousness hypothesis agree fully with his position.

The hallmark of scientific knowledge in any area is sufficient understanding of the physical principles involved to describe them in the language of mathematics. In the past, neuroscience has lacked such an understanding, and it has appeared theory-impoverished from the point of view of researchers in the hard sciences. Now, however, brain science is in the process of becoming a hard science, and it may be in roughly the place where biology was thirty years ago, when James Watson and Francis Crick first began to develop rigorous, quasi-mathematical codes for the description of the DNA molecule. The signal events in brain science's transition to a hard science were the discoveries of the brain's natural opiate receptor by Candace Pert and Solomon Snyder at Johns Hopkins in 1973, the isolation of the first natural opiate or endorphin by the Scottish scientists John Hughes and Hans Kosterlitz in 1975, and the discovery of the beta-endorphin by C. H. Li and David Chung at the University of California at San Francisco in 1976. What these researchers isolated were the first examples of molecular substances called neurotransmitters. And what made this development revolutionary is that neurotransmitters serve as basic mechanisms for information processing in the human brain. More important, the discovery of the neurotransmitters provided neuroscientists with an opportunity to develop mathematical models to describe and evaluate fundamental aspects of cognition, based on measurable and definable mechanisms.

Researchers have identified fifty neurotransmitters and are searching for more with the same zeal that quantum physicists have exhibited in their search for additional subatomic particles in high-speed particle accelerators. Part of the motivation is that which motivates all scientists: an improved understanding of the processes of nature. But the stakes in the applied aspects of this research are also enormously high. The practical benefits and consequences of the research could be quite dramatic. For example, it now appears that severe mental illness results from a chemical imbalance between three neurotransmitters—epinephrine, dopamine, and serotonin—and that effective drugs could cure schizophrenia by restoring the proper balance.[10] The same line of research could also lead to means for dealing with all forms of depression, cures for severe phobias, elimination of a host of learning and behavioral disorders, and nonaddictive, effective painkillers with minimal side effects. Neuroscientists speculate that there are as many as three hundred neurotransmitters, and that all of them will eventually be found and their precise mechanisms understood. This should be the case in spite of the fact that a single chemical can cooperate in hundreds of different bodily processes, and that these same processes may require the participation of dozens, or hundreds, of different chemicals.

The Computer as Research Tool in Neuroscience

Most of the research in neuroscience prior to the availability of the computer as a research tool involved disabling or removing some portion of a lab animal's brain and observing the impact on the animal's behavior. Assuming that the brains of other animals, principally mammals, are similar to our own, a typical experiment might involve training an animal to accomplish some task through operant conditioning, and then surgically removing a portion of the animal's brain or severing connections between gross areas of its brain. The researcher would then observe the impact of the procedure on the operantly conditioned behaviors. New drugs were tested on animal subjects by injecting lab animals with an unusually large dose of the drug, observing behavioral impacts under controlled conditions, and performing autopsies to assess gross effects of the drug on the animals' brains.

Early experiments with human subjects involved observing behavioral and cognitive changes and deficiencies in individuals who had, as a result of some accident, lost function in some portion of their brain. Surgical procedures on human subjects, like frontal lobotomies on schizophrenics and uncontrollably aggressive individuals, or severing the corpus callosum as a possible cure for severe epilepsy, also provided research opportunities. This latter procedure proved particularly useful in understanding the function and organization of the two hemispheres of the cerebral cortex.

Although progress has been made through such research, it has had its problems. The most obvious problem is that there are significant differences between the brains of laboratory animals and the human brain. For example, even research on the higher primates provides little or no opportunity to better understand the dynamics of cognitive processes involved in symbolic language, memory, and learning in our own unique cerebral cortex. A slightly different problem has been encountered in the study of human subjects with damaged brains: the results of these studies could not provide reliable insights into the actual functioning of undamaged or normal human brains. Another more recently discovered problem is that the old mechanistic model for the brain has broken down. The old model assumed that particular areas or configurations of cells were dedicated to isolated and specific functions or types of information processing, and that these areas or configurations were "wired" together and coordinated by some complicated linear information-processing network. We now know that there are considerable overlaps and redundancies in human brain function, involving dynamic and interweaving patterns in a three-dimensional space.

Removing, disabling, or manipulating chemically specific areas of the brain, and then trying to map the gross connections or interrelationships between these areas, cannot, of course, tell us anything about the dynamic and interweaving patterns present in the brains of living subjects. The computer as a research tool, however, is now enabling us to map the electrical and chemical activities of the brains of living subjects. Beginning in the 1960s, neurophysiologists began studying "event-related potentials," a means of measuring the electrical activity produced by the brain in response to various stimuli and thought processes. For example, a typical electroencephalogram (EEG) measures voltage fluctuations in the scalp through the use of electrodes. Those fluctuations are then amplified and traced as seismographic ripples on a polygraph. The ripples are a measure of the overall electromagnetic activity resulting from the firing of millions of neurons in interaction with neurotransmitters. Although a conventional EEG can detect large problems, like an epileptic seizure or serious brain damage, the random background noise of the brain's electrical activity makes it virtually impossible to precisely measure electrical responses to specific stimuli.

Researchers had previously shown that a stimulus, like a flash of light, evokes a volley of neural impulses that travel along the visual pathways of the brain. But this small electrical impulse became indecipherable in the sea of background noise generated by the general electrical activity of the brain. The problem solved by the computer was to create a window to see through the background of

randomly occurring larger wave patterns and thereby isolate or extract the evoked response. By repeating a stimulus many times, and by using a computer to sum up the
change in the background activity, the electrical turbu-
lance can be made algebraically to add to zero. With the
background activity filtered out, the waves correlating
with the stimulus become more defined: in this way the
averaging computer extracts the "evoked response" from
its background noise. As Edward Beck, a pioneer in this
research, puts it, "In a manner of speaking, the evoked
response is like a fingerprint of the brain."[11] What the
averaging computer provides is an opportunity to correlate
the amplitudes, wave shapes, and spatial distributions of
waves produced by the electrical activity of the brain with
neuronal functions that we previously had no means of
studying.

Some evidence suggests that evoked responses, or event-
related potential responses, may provide means to measure decision making, previously regarded as a complex
human variable inaccessible to neuroscience. The P300
wave, for example, has been found to be "stimulus independent," and it appears to be correlated with an intrinsic
cortical process evoked by the task demands of a situation,
rather than by specific sensory inputs. If an event seems
rare or unusual, the wave is larger or—as the researchers
put it—the P300 amplitude is "inversely related to subjective probability." The P300 wave has also been shown to
provide a reliable means of discriminating between a subject's evoked responses to nouns and verbs in language
studies. If, for example, a subject is asked to read the
sentence, "Ready, aim, fire," the P300 wave is not the
same as that produced when the subject reads the sentence, "Sit by the fire." What this suggests is that there
are mechanisms in the brain that distinguish between the
noun and verb forms in sentences. Some evidence also
suggests that an aberrant P300 wave could serve as a
genetic marker for those predisposed to alcoholism as an
inherited trait. P300 waves appear abnormally flat in alcoholics and in the sons of alcoholics.

Another class of evoked potentials, called visually evoked responses or VERs, is produced by flashing a strobe light into a subject's eyes and measuring the effect through recording electrodes placed at the back of the head in an area corresponding roughly with the location of the visual cortex. VERs on the averaging computer appear to change markedly with age and may become a means of studying the growth and aging process of the brain. Researchers have also speculated that VERs could serve as a basis for developing an IQ test that might neutralize cultural biases and differences in verbal acuity.

Another measure, known as the post-imperative negative variation (PINV), appears capable of making a differential diagnosis that often eludes the most experienced mental health professional: that between true schizophrenia and the merely schizoid personality. PINV measures are produced by requiring the subject to attend to two consecutive stimuli: a warning signal that readies the subject to perform a specific action, such as pushing a button, and a second signal indicating when the action should be performed. The first signal produces responses associated with the frontal area of the brain. After the action is carried out, however, the evoked responses indicate that the forebrain returns to its normal resting state. The amplitudes of waves produced via the averaging computer in this procedure have been shown to correlate with a variety of psychological states.

The computer as research tool in neuroscience is also being used to map the biochemical information system of the brain in a more direct fashion. The original research on the neurotransmitters used a method called radioactive tagging. In order to discover the receptor sites for a putative neurotransmitter, researchers combined a substance like naloxone with a radioactive substance and injected them into the brain of an experimental animal. The animal was then killed, and its brain was removed and placed in a radioactive counter. The highest counts of radioactivity could be expected in the areas of the brain where the receptors are located. This experiment could not, of course, provide a great deal of detailed information about the human brain. And the procedure also could not provide a dynamic view of neurotransmitter mechanisms in living subjects.

There is now, however, a computer-based technology, known as the positron emission tomography (PET) scanner, that provides a color-enhanced view of this dynamic process. After radioactive fluorine is introduced into the patient's body and absorbed into the brain, the scanner builds a picture of events in the brain as the radioactive material decays and emits positrons—positively charged electrons—that collide with negatively charged electrons in the surrounding tissue. The collisions create two gamma rays which exit from the brain tissue at 180-degree angles. Radiation-sensitive cameras detect these rays, and this data is communicated to a large computer that constructs a metabolic map of the activities of the subject's brain. Since the cells that are firing the fastest require more glucose, the PET scan allows researchers to watch as the brain metabolizes its energy source into the electrical and chemical processes we know as thoughts and emotions.

This research tool has already revealed, for example, specific brain sites that appear to malfunction in patients suffering from severe depression, anxiety, and schizophrenia—as well as a good deal about the action and interaction of neurotransmitters at those sites. The PET scan has allowed us to better understand how various drugs metabolize and act on specific brain sites. Antidepressants, for example, work on the planning and organizing patterns generated in the frontal lobe, and neuroleptic drugs, used to treat schizophrenia, travel to a cluster of cells that forms the connective link between spine and brain called the basal ganglia. The PET scan is also providing new insights into the dynamic activity of the brain in normal subjects as they engage in various mental activities. If a subject is asked, for example, to do mental arithmetic, the parietal cortex typically becomes more active. Yet a different part of the parietal area becomes active if the same subject imagines walking down one of the streets near his or her home. If the subject is asked to summon up the appearance of his or her living room, the middle part of the midfrontal cortex is activated.

In theory, any neurotransmitter can be visualized by a PET scan if a radioactively labeled chemical can be customized to make a molecular fit. Ligands, as these substances are called, are now being developed for the benzodiazepine, serotonin, and histamine receptors, and for one type of receptor for acetylcholine. What all of this is leading toward, suggests Candace Pert, now at NIMH, is a "color-coded wiring diagram of the brain. A color-coded map, with blue for one neurochemical, red for another, and so on. We'll be able to describe the brain in mathematical, neurochemical, and electrical terms, with all the rigor of a differential equation."[12] Other diagnostic and computer-based research tools similar to the PET scanner are the brain electrical activity mapping system (BEAM), computerized axial tomography (CAT), and nuclear magnetic resonance (NMR) (see Figure 4).

Although we have only begun to explore the potential of these technologies to disclose the physical substrates of human consciousness, all indications are that progress will be rapid. The computer has become a vitally important research tool in neuroscience, a tool that is allowing us to expand our knowledge of the actual mechanisms of brain function exponentially. What is not as widely known is that this knowledge is almost immediately exploited by cognitive scientists in an effort to build computer systems modeled, however crudely at this point, after the internal organization and functions of the human brain. Equally significant, computers with architectures based on knowledge derived from neuroscience are almost immediately put to work as research tools in neuroscience. What we confront here is a classic example of a feedback loop— advances in scientific knowledge lead to the creation of new technologies which become research tools that allow for additional extensions and refinements of scientific knowledge.

Figure 4 Results of Computer-Based Research in Neuroscience

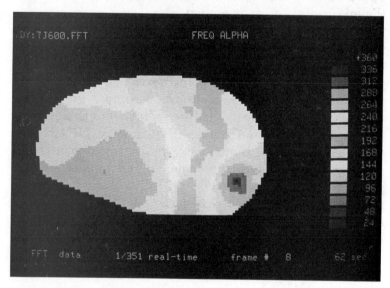

Computer-generated EEG map.

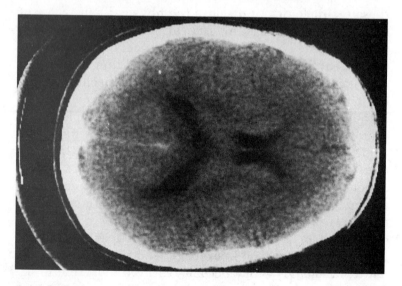

Axial CAT scan.

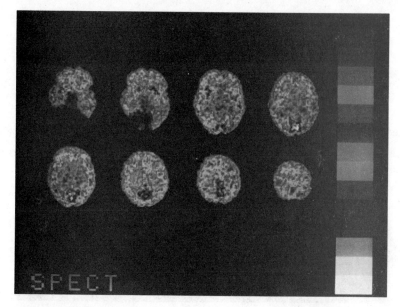

8-slice SPECT scan.

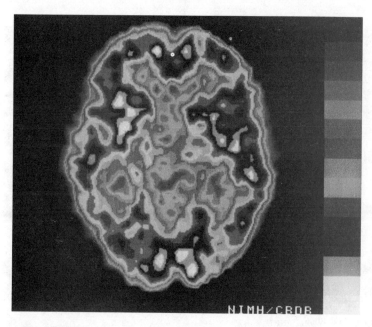

1-slice SPECT scan.

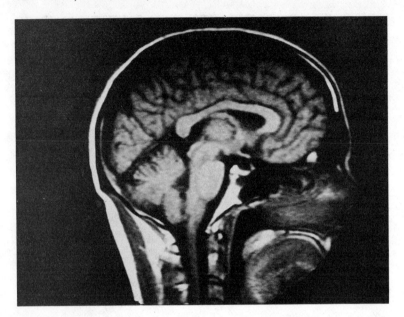

Sarital NMR scan.

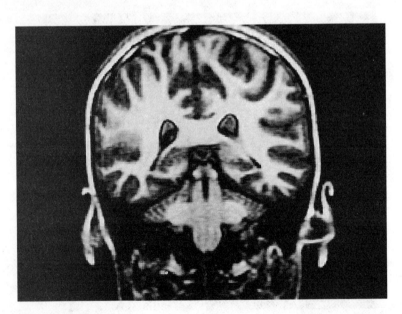

Coronal NMR scan.

The Connectionists Program

Since the time of ENIAC, virtually all computers have featured Von Neumann architectures, and most of the increased speed and computational ability of the computer has come from advances in chip technology. If the brain were a Von Neumann computer, it would have a central processing unit (CPU), random-access memory (RAM), disk storage, and busses linking all the components together. The human brain does its processing via large numbers of neuronal units that generate complex patterns of information in a parallel, as opposed to a serial, manner. If we are dealing with a problem whose solution has an orderly and predictable structure, the linear processing of Von Neumann computers is well suited to the task. But when the solution to the problem calls for associative reasoning, the need to make best-case approximations, or the manipulation of information and symbols that are "fuzzy" or that overlap one another in different contextual frames, traditional computers are not ideally suited to the task.

Aware of the limitations of Von Neumann architectures, cognitive scientists are developing computer architectures featuring large numbers of parallel processing units in the effort to approximate the organization and function of the "wet machine." In a world in which events do not take place in a conveniently serial fashion, the human brain is adept at dealing with a vast number of separate objects and processes in parallel. Pioneers in parallel processing, who tend to refer to themselves as "connectionists," are rapidly developing computer systems designed to solve problems that are irregular, unpredictable, and governed by rules that are not universal. Inspired by the brain's neural network, the connectionists emphasize massive parallelism, distributed information storage, and associative interconnections. At least fifty major research efforts in this country alone are dedicated to building new parallel computer systems.

The computers whose architectures most closely model our present understanding of the organization and function of the human brain are called neural nets. The appearance of neural nets signals the beginning of what we have already begun to call a revolution—and not only because they are potentially more capable of complex problem solving in areas involving the "fuzzy" business of evaluation. An impressive number of cognitive scientists are seeking to represent the behavior of actual neurons and circuits by modeling these neurons and circuits on neural nets. These experiments have already proven that neural nets are capable of emulating aspects of brain function and have provided startling new insights into the underlying or emergent structures of actual brain function. Neural nets are now being used to model a wide range of information-processing activities in the human brain, ranging from smell to vision to language acquisition to decision making featuring best-case approximations and associative reasoning.

If this research program leads to the development of a mathematical model that discloses how interactions at the level of the synapse generate widely distributed and redundant neuronal patterns, this would represent a giant step forward in the effort to create a conscious computer by the Turing criteria. Assuming that we do arrive at a detailed scientific description of the physical substrates of human consciousness, many computer scientists are convinced that technological barriers will not prevent us from emulating the dynamics of this consciousness on a computer system. Although there are some computer scientists who are concerned that insuperable technological barriers could prevent us from constructing a computer that can pass the Turing test, technologies in the nascent stage of development could remove any such barriers over the next few decades. A number of technologies already in the research and development phase could serve to resolve the number of units problem, the connections problem, the massively parallel architecture problem, the multivalued-logics problem, the speed problem, and so on.

In order to view these developments as I intend to view them, one must first assume that the movement toward the creation of a conscious computer by the Turing criteria will be so rapid as to obviate any comparisons with the gradual and incremental process via which the human brain evolved in Darwinian evolution. The conscious computer will not, of course, come into existence as a result of random changes in its DNA which may or may not prove useful in the quest for survival. The evolution of this intelligence will be in accordance with conscious design, and learned behaviors will be transferred from one generation to the next. Equally important, we can also anticipate that dramatic technological breakthroughs, like those witnessed with the appearance of transistors, integrated circuits, and VLSI circuits, will speed this progress along considerably. If we also assume that this progress will involve convergence, or synergism, between the emergent consciousness of AI computers and the information-processing system of the human brain, then major breakthroughs in computer-based research in neuroscience could result in exponential leaps in the ability of AI systems to emulate more aspects of actual brain function.

AI Systems as Our Most Important Product

When we confront the prospect that new technologies could alter the balance of power between nations, radically restructure the character of our daily lives, or impact the manner in which we perceive or structure our realities, our usual tendency is to quickly opt for the progress that closely correlates in our experience with increases in economic and geopolitical power. What makes this tendency more than a little problematic in the technological era we are now entering is that business as usual will feature a new relationship to our most important products: AI computer systems. The most significant aspect of new AI systems will not be their ability to better emulate aspects of the human sensorium, like manipulating objects in three-dimensional space in robotics. Nor will it be their capacity to function as "experts" in coordinating a broad new range of activities in production systems and in the management of computer-based information. The most significant aspect of the coming generations of AI systems is that they will be able to make best-case appproximations based on a large number of variables in different contextual frameworks, or to deal with what are known as the "fuzzy" problems of valuation. In the view of their developers at least, the AI systems that will quickly become capable of dealing with such problems are neural nets. The design, or architecture, of neural nets, modeled after an improved understanding of the neuronal organization and function of the human brain, allows these systems to compute solutions to fuzzy problems in ways that are clearly analogous to how the human brain computes solutions to a wide range of problems.

Since the neural-net revolution is so recent, these systems have not as yet proven themselves vastly more capable of handling the fuzzy problems of valuation than AI programs running on traditional Von Neumann architectures. The reasons why the researchers and developers of neural-net computers are convinced that these systems will prove themselves far more capable of dealing with such problems than computers with traditional architectures will be dealt with in some detail later. The principal role played by computer technologies thus far has been to store, process, and manage information. If the predictions of the developers of neural-net systems are correct, however, this situation is about to change very rapidly.

These theorists claim that the coming generations of neural-net computers will be capable of valuation and decision making based on the analysis of complex variables in contextual frameworks that cannot be readily dealt with in terms of binary, either-or, or monotonic logic. If this occurs, and there is some solid evidence suggesting that it will, then neural-net computers could soon become actors in roles that have been previously played only by human beings. In the more distant future, it is also likely that computer systems will be capable of performing virtually any single or dedicated task faster and more efficiently than human beings. This means that at some point during the first half of the next century, these systems could become the ultimate repository of assumptions, attitudes, values, and modes of analysis in the management and control of major societal systems and organizations. And it is also conceivable that during the same time frame consciousness as defined by the Turing criteria will eventually become an emergent property of the internal organization and design of AI computers.

Whether this last prospect becomes a reality is obviously open to debate, and there are members of the AI community who view it with large measures of skepticism. These skeptics are quick to point out that the mindlike capabilities that have been attributed to AI systems are vastly overblown. And there are points in this discussion where I will demonstrate that this is, in fact, the case. Yet when one attempts to chart the progress that can reasonably be made in AI computer technologies in the foreseeable future, it is not difficult to conclude that the vision of the technological future advanced by the advocates of the AI evolution-of-consciousness hypothesis seems to have a good deal of substantive validity. However, if that vision does become a reality, it will not be for the reasons advanced by the advocates of the hypothesis.

At the moment there appears to be one rather lonely voice among AI experts urging us to recognize the invidious character of the AI evolution-of-consciousness hypothesis. According to Joseph Weizenbaum at MIT, the hypothesis represents "a great absurdity and also a dangerous absurdity because in a certain sense it lays a philosophical and scientific foundation for a genocide on the entire human species." What we are witnessing here is nothing less, he suggests, than the "beginning of justification for the elimination of the human gene pool."[13] What most horrifies Weizenbaum about those who advocate the hypothesis is that they refuse to recognize that human life and consciousness based on the biological substrate of Darwinian evolution are the "ultimate value," and that nothing would be left after that value is destroyed. This ultimate value is the central character in this book, and yet protecting and preserving it in the technological future will be, as I hope to demonstrate, no easy task.

CHAPTER 2

The Mind Is Its Own Place: The Human Brain as Reality Processor

A great disorder is an order. Now, A
And B are not like statuary, posed
For a visit in the Louvre. They are things
chalked
On the sidewalk so that the pensive man may
see.

—Wallace Stevens
"Connoisseur of Chaos"

In the 1940s, when theorists like Turing first conceived of the prospect of constructing a conscious computer, the theorists were operating on two related assumptions that research in neuroscience eventually proved to be false. The first assumption, deeply embedded in Western intellectual tradition since the ancient Greek philosophers, was that consciousness is most closely associated with reason, or with grammatical and logical constructions in language. It was this assumption in the seventeenth century that led Leibniz to propose that philosophers should devote themselves to constructing a *Characteristica Universalis*, or a universal calculus of human thought. Leibniz's hypothesis was further refined in the nineteenth century, when a number of logicians suggested that symbolic logic was logically prior to mathematics, and that this logic could decode the fundamental dynamics of human cognition.

Believing in the validity of this assumption, George Boole, a self-taught mathematician, attempted to divide the world into two classes and to define operations that could be performed on the two classes. In his *Investigation into the Laws of Thought, on which Are Founded the Mathematical Theories of Logic and Possibilities*, Boole defined the classes as *p* and *q*, or 0 and 1. A string of 0s and 1s could, he suggested, function as the equivalent of propositional calculus, or as a code for representing a logical series of operations based on if-then statements. The importance of Boole's work for the technological future became apparent in 1937, when Claude Shannon, then a graduate student at MIT, demonstrated that complex electrical circuits could operate in two states which could be manipulated in terms of Boolean algebra and binary arithematic.

The second related assumption that led figures like Turing to imagine that a mindlike computer was a technological possibility was that the fundamental mechanisms of the human brain could be described in terms of Boolean logic. Neurophysiologist Warren S. McCulloch and mathematician Walter Pitts concluded in 1943 that electrical signals pass along the axon and trigger chemical processes in the brain that cause a neighboring neuron to react in terms of two states: firing or not firing. If the universal calculus of human thought was Boolean logic, then the next obvious conclusion was that all of the mechanisms of human thought could be emulated on complex computer systems. Another important conceptual ingredient here was a notion developed five years later by Norbert Wiener. In *Cybernetics*, Wiener proposed that the goal-oriented, purposeful behavior of the human brain could be explained in terms of the mathematics of feedback and feedforward. The first major attempt to construct a pseudo-brain out of electrical circuits was made at Cornell University shortly thereafter.[1]

It would soon be discovered that neurons were not as simple in their behavior as McCulloch and Pitts supposed, and that Boolean logic could not simulate all aspects of human brain function. The electrical responses at the synapse are nonlinear and involve enormously complex chemical interactions in addition to electrical processes. The special character of the interactions at the synapse also results in more global functions that are highly distributed and redundant. Yet many cognitive scientists are confident that a conscious computer could be built if the actual mechanisms via which the biological computer processes its information were understood. If there are barriers to the construction of such a computer, it is probable, in my view, that they will not be technological. The fundamental breakthrough that now seems required in order to accomplish this technological feat is a theoretical model that describes the global aspects of brain function in mathematical, or full scientific, detail.

The Human Brain as Information-Processing System

All large information-processing systems, including the organic system that is our brain, function hierarchically. Elements of neural information, generated by changes of state in individual nerve cells, are combined into subroutines within higher-level programs that ultimately control or direct human experience and behavior. Environmental information in the form of physical energy—light or photons, movement of molecules in the air, chemicals that reach sensory surfaces, mechanical deformation of the skin, inertial changes of bodily fluid, etc.—is transformed by sense cells into neural code. The initial transformation of information from energy to neural code is made in peripheral parts of the visual, auditory, olfactory and gustatory (chemical), tactile, and proprioceptive (muscles, tissues, and joints) systems. Very different kinds of physical information become represented as a neural code of action potentials and as waves of polarization and depolarization.

Virtually all the tasks that seem hard or difficult for human beings but that the present generation of computers can easily perform are associated with the neuronal organization of parts of our brain that are quite new in evolutionary terms. Conversely, tasks that human beings normally view as easy but that are difficult to even begin to emulate on computers have a much longer evolutionary history. Although playing chess, doing higher mathematics, making medical diagnoses, and troubleshooting electronic circuits may seem intellectually challenging for human beings, computer systems can meet the challenge very nicely. If the computer seems a bit moronic when its abilities to see its environment or coordinate movements are compared to those of a normal two-year-old child, it is because the child is making use of multiple levels of processing ability that have been evolving for thousands, or even millions, of years.

The neuronal organization of the human brain came into existence at a quite leisurely pace. Four billion years of Darwinian evolution led in this instance to the creation of an information-processing system that is staggering in its complexity. As the famous neuroscientist Sir Charles Sherrington put it, "The human brain is an enchanted loom where millions of flashing shuttles weave a dissolving pattern, always a meaningful pattern, though never an abiding one. It is as if the Milky Way entered upon some cosmic dance."[2] When Sherrington wrote these lines in the mid-1940s, the mechanisms through which the enchanted loom created, projected, or wove its reality were still quite mysterious and, like all great mysteries, best described in the language of poetry. Although our present scientific description certainly has not eliminated or explained the mysterious in brain function, we are now in the process of discovering, with the aid of research tools provided by advanced computer technologies, the underlying physical principles and mechanisms involved.

What the present generation of computers clearly cannot do is function as an "enchanted loom," or create its own realities infused with will, purpose, awareness, and understanding. Computers are not "conscious" as we are conscious, nor do they have a sense of "self" as an intellectual and emotional entity that acts and reacts to the world of its being. Although the experience of "self" as we now understand it in neuroscience involves myriad parallel processes in the brain, our conscious conceptions of self derive largely from our ability to acquire and use natural language or complex symbol systems generally. Our own evolutionary history was such that it predisposed us to invent and refine those systems. As NIMH neuroscientist Paul MacLean has pointed out, human language as a cognitive system encumbers large amounts of neural tissue, whereas communication in most species involves little such tissue.[3] Behavior in other organisms, even complex behavior, requires little brain tissue to control. The business of creating a symbolic reality via the human sensory-perceptual systems demands, in contrast, a large investment of neural processing capacity.

The neuronal organization of the human brain that allowed us to invent and develop the symbol system of natural language is a fairly recent evolutionary development, and it coexists with other systems that are a part of our shared biological inheritance as vertebrates. Some of these relatively primitive systems are capable of registering experiences and regulating behavior largely outside of any conscious awareness (see Figure 5). The human brain is a kind of archeological site, with the outer layer composed of the most recent brain structure, the cerebral cortex, and the deeper layers consisting of structures from our shared evolutionary history with the reptiles and mammals. MacLean likens these three brains to "biological computers, each having its own intelligence, its own subjectivity, its own sense of time and space, and its own memory and other functions."[4]

Figure 5 Human Brain Structure

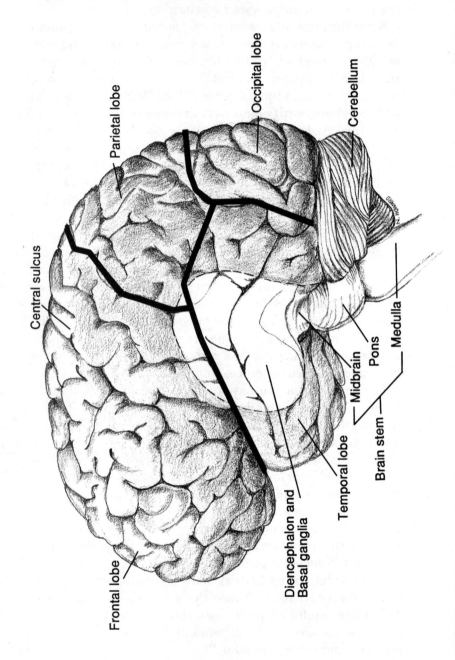

In evolutionary terms, all brains are extensions of the spinal cord, and the shared history of our brains with those of reptiles and mammals is evident in a characteristic three-segmented shape. The first segment swells into the medulla (controlling breathing, heart rate, digestion), the cerebellum (coordinating senses and muscle movements), and pons (relays for breathing, hearing, feeding, movement, and facial expressions). This knobby portion of all brains is known as the lower brain stem. The second segment appears as a slight swelling in lower vertebrates and enlarges in the higher primates and ourselves into midbrain structures. These structures link the lower brain stem to the thalamus, for information relay, and to the hypothalamus, which is instrumental in regulating drives and actions. The third segment, the forebrain, appears as a bump or nodule in the brain of a frog, balloons into the cerebrum of higher life forms, and covers the brain stem like the head of a mushroom. It further evolved in ourselves into the walnutlike configuration of left and right hemispheres which, in contrast to those of the higher primates, have specialized functions (see Figure 6).

The Neocortex: Crowning Glory

The human neocortex looks like a redundantly folded sheet about three millimeters thick, and it is divided into two hemispheres that function like two fairly independent brains or two parallel processors. Although the symmetry between the two hemispheres is not exact, the structures on one side are mirrored by structures on the other. Thus we have two frontal lobes, two temporal lobes, two parietal lobes, two occipital lobes, and so on. In our species the neocortex contains at least 70 percent of the neurons in the central nervous system, and its various regions are highly specialized. Ridges and indentations, known as gyri and sulci, mark the boundaries between regions in the cortex, and the grossest lines of demarcation are between the four lobes. The two occipital lobes, located toward the back of

Figure 6 Human Brain Structure

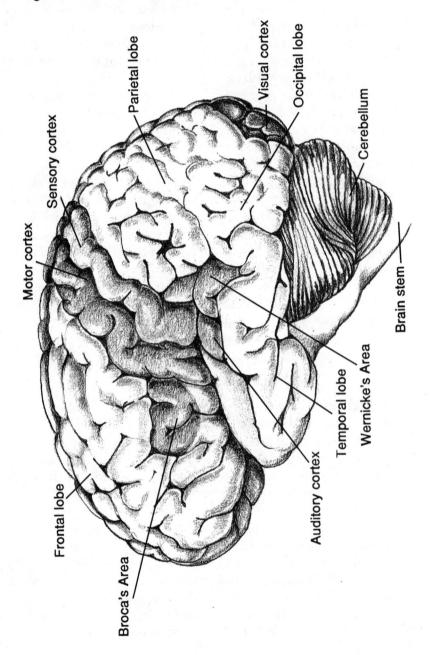

the head, are associated with the primary visual area. The temporal lobes, located right above the ear on both sides of the head, are intimately connected with the limbic system that lies below, and are also associated with a primary auditory area. Also, some visual messages processed through the occipital lobe have been discovered to feed back to the temporal lobe. The parietal lobes, which arch over the brain from roughly ear to ear, contain a kind of schematic map of the body, or rather two topographic maps in which areas are associated with motor and somatosensory, or tactile, responses. Every inch of the body is represented in an organized fashion on the cortex (see Figure 7).

The two frontal lobes occupy the front part of the brain behind the forehead and compose the portion of the brain most closely associated with "control" or "read out" of responses based on feedback from the entire neuronal organization. In most people, the left hemisphere takes dominance over the right in deciding which response will be made. Since the frontal lobes occupy 29 percent of the cortex in our species—as opposed to 3.5 percent in rats and 17 percent for chimpanzees—they are often regarded as an index of our evolutionary advancement. "If God speaks to man, if man speaks to God," comments neuroscientist Candace Pert, "it would be through the frontal lobes, which is the part of the brain that has undergone the most recent evolutionary expansion."[5]

Searching for the Neural Code

These structural features of the brain have been known for some time, and the same is true of the gross structure of the neurons. But knowledge of how environmental stimuli are translated into neural code, as a result of synaptic transmission and related cellular processes, is quite recent. Part of the problem has been to decipher how an electrical potential is generated in one cell and then travels along its axon at a constant rate and coded sequence.

Figure 7 Human Brain Structure

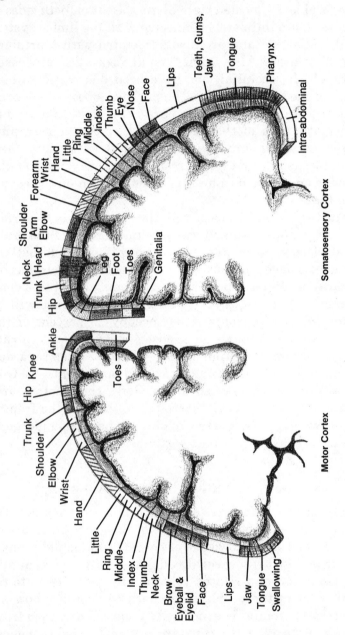

Along the length of the axon the process is purely electrical. It is when the signal reaches the end of the axon, and the information must be transferred across the gap or synaptic cleft between axons, that the neurotransmitters are released.

The code here is decipherable on the level of the molecular structure of the neurotransmitters, which link to specific receptor sites in the neighboring neuron. A neurotransmitter exerts either an excitatory effect on the target neuron, causing it to fire, or an inhibitory effect, preventing it from firing. It acts by altering the permeability of the receptor cell membrane, and thereby affects the voltage within the cell. This is not, however, a simple on-off process—it is graded, like a dimmer control, and requires a certain strength to have an effect. If a neuron forms a network with other neurons, its axons will have many branches, with each branch storing a neurotransmitter that connects with a specific target cell.

One of the first dramatic demonstrations in neuroscience of the enormous capabilities of the human brain as an information storage and retrieval system was provided by experiments conducted in the 1940s and 1950s. At McGill University, neurosurgeon William Penfield and his colleague Herbert Jasper designed experiments that involved the electrical stimulation of the exposed brains of patients undergoing neurosurgery under local anesthetic. Thus the patients were fully awake and alert during the procedure. A stimulating electrode applied to the temporal lobes of these patients frequently evoked a reexperiencing in memory of isolated and often seemingly unimportant, or trivial, events from the past. More remarkably, the memory seemed so complete and intense that the patients felt that they were back in that earlier time hearing, seeing, and feeling everything as it was originally experienced. Yet the patients were also aware that these strange mental experiences did not correspond to any real events taking place in the operating room. It was as if two selves

Figure 8 Human Limbic System

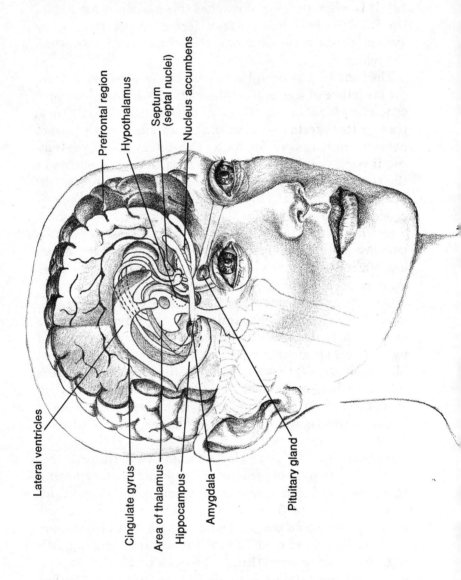

were active in this moment of cognition: the self that was reliving the experience in the past, and the self that was aware of its existence in the present and reporting on that past experience.

These and other experiments like them illustrate the following: (1) the human brain seemingly has the capacity to record vast amounts of information in memory; (2) what is recorded has a fully developed emotional dimension; (3) memory involves both localized and more general or global regions of the brain; and (4) an observing self in the present coexists, in some sense, with the self that reexperiences the past event. More recently, psychologists Elizabeth and Geoffrey Loftus reexamined Penfield's results and concluded that the recalls, based on the evidence from experiments on 1,132 cortical-stimulation patients, resembled reconstructions of earlier events, rather than the actual reliving of those events.[6] But even this caveat does not discount the fact that the brain is capable of recording large amounts of information, even when this information is woven into a plausible or coherent story as opposed to a totally faithful recollection of events as they actually occurred.

Studies of the neural pathways of information transfer in the human brain have already begun to reveal the mechanisms informing or underlying these dynamic systems. The most important brain stucture associated with emotion is the limbic system. A number of structures in the brain stem and parts of the cortex are also intimately involved. The limbic system, essentially alike in all mammals, sits above the brain stem and under the cortex and consists of a number of interconnected structures. Brain and behavior experts have linked these interconnecting structures to hormones, drives, temperature control, reward and punishment centers, and one part, the hippocampus, to memory formation (see Figure 8). Certain nuclei in the anterior thalamus are part of the alliance, and under that gland lies the small but potent hypothalamus.

Neurons affecting the activities of the autonomic nervous system—heart rate, respiration, etc.—appear concentrated in the hypothalamus and direct most of the physiological changes that accompany strong emotion. The amygdala, which lies deep in the lateral brain and is roughly the size of a walnut, is active in the production of aggressive behavior and fearful reactions. It also appears responsible for adding positive associations to specific stimuli.

Adjacent to the amygdala is the hippocampus, which is closely connected with the search for novelty. The destruction of the hippocampus in a lab animal, for example, will cause the animal to return monotonously to the areas of the cage already explored and to ignore unexplored regions. The hippocampus is also responsible for integrating various forms of incoming information, particularly as part of the dynamics of long-term memory, and for making and storing spatial maps. Damage to both the amygdala and hippocampus will produce global retrograde amnesis, or the inability to lay down new stores of information.

Encircling the hippocampus and the other structures of the limbic system is the cingulate gyrus (meaning "girdling" or "encircling") which connects to a two-way fiber system called the fornix. MacLean's research has led him to the conclusion that the cingulate gyrus is the source of behaviors we identify with mammals and not with reptiles: nursing, or maternal care, play, and audiovocal communication. The fornix follows the curve of the cingulate gyrus and connects the hippocampus to the hypothalamus. Another structure, the septum, receives neural input through the fornix from the hippocampus and sends neural output to the hypothalamus. The hypothalamus, which also regulates blood pressure, body temperature, and appetite, controls emotional states and responses by regulating the output of chemicals from the glands. The septum is associated with intense pleasure, such as orgasm, and patients implanted with electrodes in this region will self-stimulate repeatedly.

Following the course of the neural pathways, we begin to see why all of our interactions and memories have an emotional coloring or quality. Incoming neural messages from all of the senses travel through pathways in the brain stem, the various processing levels in the cortex, or both, and then pass through one or more of the limbic structures: the amygdala, the hippocampus, or part of the thalamus. Throughout these pathways the continually processed and reprocessed neural codes travel as electrical codes in the axon and biochemical codes in the neurotransmitters. The neurotransmitters essentially bring us coded information from the outside world, and the receptors determine how we respond to that information. If the polarization across cell membranes is altered, then the signals neurons send to other neurons are altered. Thus a chain of minute electrical events ensues that may culminate in rage, fear, grief, caring, or any number of emotional states and behaviors.[7] What is particularly interesting to cognitive scientists is that emotions are never neutral, and that they present themselves in one of two states: agreeable or disagreeable. This insight has been incorporated into the theoretical models of some AI theorists in order to explain the manner in which emotion could emerge as an internal dynamic of complex computer systems based on neural-net architectures.

One aspect of brain function that we have already begun to emulate on neural-net computers is the dynamics of short- and long-term memory. Short-term memory is an active process of limited duration and leaves no traces, while long-term memory is produced by structural changes in the neuronal system. The most widely held hypothesis suggests that structural changes result from repeated activation of a loop of neurons that run from the cortex to the thalamus or hippocampus and back to the cortex. Once connected, these neurons would constitute a "cell assembly," and any excitation of a critical number of cells in the assembly would activate the whole assembly. In this way a memory could be stored and retrieved by any sensation, thought, or emotion that activated a critical number of the neurons in the assembly. The structural changes are believed to occur at the synapses, and thereby increase one neuron's effect on a neighboring neuron.[8] What is clearly indicated by these and other models from neuroscience is that learning and memory are active processes in which a hierarchy of evolving patterns are coincident with the storage and retrieval of knowledge. A pattern that does not repeat would become a short-term memory that might be stored for only a few seconds to several minutes. Repetition of the dynamic pattern would reinforce and enlarge its associations, and would result in the gradual emergence of a long-term memory that could be stored from several hours to a lifetime.

As we discover more neurotransmitters, follow their production and pathways through brain sites, and understand more about the mechanisms within the cells themselves, the map of actual brain function will become increasingly more complete. But this map will not reveal a point-to-point correspondence between particular areas of the brain and aspects of the reality constructed by the brain. For example, many regions of the brain, in addition to the cerebral cortex, are critical to learning, and memories within the cortex appear highly distributed and redundant. In computer terms the brain appears to be a massively parallel network, and it is this structure that allows for its great redundancy as well as its fault tolerance. Knowledge in the biological computer appears distributed throughout the network; it is not localized in the equivalent of a specific magnetic memory core or the position of a microswitch. Since this knowledge seems distributed along the strengths of connections between the units, the brain does not appear as much to "compute" a solution as to "settle into" a solution as a result of massive parallel processing. In this distributed system there is no "center," and so-called brain areas are merely terms representing extrinsic connections to other features of the dynamic process.

Split-Brain Research

In order to create a conscious computer, it is necessary to better understand the relationship between the quite different information-processing styles of the two hemispheres of the brain. The most crucial information provided thus far comes from split-brain research. In 1967, Dr. Roger Sperry at the California Institute of Technology reported results on sixteen patients who had undergone a radical surgical procedure to control life-threatening seizures. The procedure involved severing the corpus callosum—a 200-million fiber network connecting the left and right hemispheres of the brain—in the hope of confining seizure discharges to only one hemisphere. Sperry realized that this was a unique opportunity to learn more about the specialized functions of the hemispheres. Here is his summary of the most remarkable conclusion:

> The most interesting and striking features of the syndrome of hemisphere disconnection may be summarized as an apparent doubling in most of the realms of conscious awareness. Instead of the normally unified single stream of consciousness, these patients behave in many ways as if they have two independent streams of conscious awareness, one in each hemisphere, each of which is cut off from and out of contact with the mental experiences of the other. In other words, each hemisphere seems to have its own separate and private sensations, its own perceptions, its own private impulses to act. . . . Following the surgery, each hemisphere also has, therefore, its own separate chain of memories that are rendered inaccessible to the recall process of the other.[9]

In normal subjects, information is processed in either the left or the right hemisphere, and the results are then communicated to the other hemisphere via the corpus callosum. In the split-brain patients, each hemisphere operated in isolation. This situation provided researchers with an opportunity to determine what specialized functions occur in the two hemispheres prior to the point at which they share the processed information.

Consider the following experiment conducted by Sperry: Two different figures were projected on a screen at a speed of less than one-tenth of a second, much too fast for a subject to shift eye fixation and pick up the image in both visual fields. Thus everything to the left of the central visual fixation point was processed by the right hemisphere, and everything to the right by the left hemisphere. In one typical experiment a dollar sign was flashed to the left and a question mark to the right. The subject, who had the split-brain operation, was asked to draw what he saw using his left hand. The subject then immediately drew the dollar sign with his left hand, which was controlled by the brain's right hemisphere. If the subject was then asked what he had just drawn, he would respond, "A question mark." The explanation for this discrepancy is that speech in most people is confined to the left hemisphere, and the verbal knowledge that the subject had of the experimental situation was in that hemisphere. In contrast, the dollar sign that the right hemisphere recognized and drew with the left hand existed not as verbal knowledge, but rather as knowledge in a picture that could be reproduced. But in the split-brain patients, the speech-dominant left hemisphere did not have this knowledge— thus the patient drew one thing but verbally identified a different thing.

What the split-brain research revealed was that each of the hemispheres in the human brain has its own cognitive style. In individuals with normal hemispheric dominance, the left hemisphere, which manages the right half of the body, controls language and general cognitive functions. The right hemisphere, which controls the left half of the body, manages nonverbal processes, such as attention, subtle pattern discrimination, line orientation, and the detection of complex auditory tones. One large difference between the two hemispheres is that the normally dominant left appears to be a kind of "inference engine" that interprets overt behaviors as well as more covert emotional responses from other brain regions. The right hemisphere, which is incapable in split-brain research of solving simple math problems or geometric puzzles that would be easy for most second graders, appears, in contrast, to play a minimal role in directing, interpreting, and rationalizing behaviors. Although in normal subjects the two hemispheres constantly communicate with one another, acting as parallel processors with complementary functions, the dominant left hemisphere specializes in functions most closely associated with the self as actor in human reality.

Human Brain as Massively Parallel Modular System

As the American psychologist William James demonstrated in the early decades of this century, there is a large difference between the view of consciousness as a unified and logically constructed system and the actual experience of consciousness in our subjective reality. Consciousness as we experience it, prior to any effort to represent the content of consciousness in language, is clearly a "stream" of memory fragments, verbal and nonverbal images, emotional states, bodily sensations, fantasies, perceptual data, and so on. Any sense that we have of our self as a logical and self-consistent entity is a function of the abstract symbol system of language. Although James's views may have seemed a bit radical when they were first published, they have since become rather commonplace. It requires little imagination to conclude that our actual experience of self on the subjective level does not seem amenable to being represented in any known logical system. Thus any idea we may have of the self as unified and logically consistent is not commensurate with the full range of conscious experience. Rather, any idea of the self is a partial and necessarily distorted representation of the full experience of consciousness as expressed in linguistic and cultural codes. Since the experience of consciousness on the primary subjective level seems ineffable and alogical, it would appear that there is no way in which consciousness on this primary level could be emulated by a computer system. Thus, any computer system that might seem "conscious" could not in principle emulate the full range of human consciousness.

Although this could well be the case for some time, neuroscience has developed a new model for the global organization of the brain that suggests that our experience of consciousness in subjective reality as ineffable and mysterious may eventually be disclosed to scientific understanding. Presuming that this new model leads to a more detailed understanding of the interrelated functions of various brain regions, there is no reason why we could not eventually construct a computer system that would apprehend its own "consciousness" in subjective reality as fundamentally ineffable and mysterious as well. The model, developed by neuroscientist Michael Gazzaniga, assumes that the brain is organized "into relatively independent functioning units that work in parallel,"[10] and that it does not, therefore, operate as an indivisible whole.

In Gazzaniga's model, the brain is not a single integrated system that gives rise to a unified cognitive process based on a serial or linear architecture. Instead, it is organized in "modules" that process information in quasi-independent fashion. As Gazzaniga puts it, the human brain "is more a sociological entity than a psychological entity. That is, the human brain is composed of a vast number of more elementary units, and many of these units are capable of carrying out rather sophisticated mental work."[11] What is most significant here is that much of this mental work occurs outside of the awareness of the verbal consciousness system, or, put differently, extensive information processing goes on independently of the information processing done by verbal systems. In computer terms, this means that the brain is a massively parallel network, within which functions at various levels of the

hierarchy can be performed redundantly and in a quasi-
autonomous fashion. If human consciousness seems ineffable and mysterious on the primary subjective level, Gazzaniga suggests that it may be because the relatively independent processing modules of the brain represent
multiple aspects of the entire information-processing system—aspects that the verbal processing system is either
not aware of or cannot "read out."

The verbal processing system displays a powerful compulsion to maintain a sense of consistency for all behaviors. It is this compulsion that seems to explain why the
verbal processing system is capable of overriding inputs
from the powerful limbic system. Similarly, if actual behaviors are not consistent with conceptions of consistent
behavior, the verbal processing system is capable of rationalizing the behavior to allow for more consistency and
even of refashioning a remembered event to achieve more
consistency. If Gazzaniga's model is correct, then the "observing self" disclosed in Penfield's experiments could be
the verbal processing module in action. Since the verbal
processing module can represent the totality of inputs
from other brain modules only in terms of its own logic or
its own culturally derived sense of coherence, it makes its
inferences based on those inputs that can be made subject
to that sense of coherence. Gazzaniga's model also provides a very different basis for understanding the dynamics of the neuronal patterns of the brain that Freud labeled
the unconscious. Within the modular view, the unconscious is represented as "coconscious but nonverbal mental
modules."[12]

What is most significant for our purposes is that this
understanding of the dynamic structure of the human
brain from neuroscience has become the basis for constructing new AI computer systems with alternate architectures. A number of AI experts have drawn upon this
model to suggest that consciousness could be an emergent
property of a massively parallel computer system, a sys-

tem in which processing modules operate fairly independently of one another at various levels in the hierarchical organization. In theory, in the coming generations of AI systems the totality of inputs from all subordinate modules could emerge in the hierachy of organization at a level corresponding to human subjective reality. At this level, the subordinate inputs would be acted upon or processed by inference-making modules that determine read outs associated with the "conscious" content of the system. Theorists also suggest that the various modules contributing information to the level where the system will begin to read out its conclusions will operate on multivalued logics and in terms of connections that are not simply binary. Similarly, the read-out mechanisms will, they claim, be based on multivalued logics and interconnections that make "best case" approximations, or that can deal with the "fuzzy" problems of valuation.

Although new AI systems built on such architectures may eventually display a dazzling new range of capabilities, it is just as likely that, in the absence of a much-improved understanding of brain function, they will not be able to rival the capacities of the human brain. The aspects of brain function that we most critically need to understand in order to build a more mindlike computer are the manner in which cell-to-cell connections code information differently in the various modules, and the manner in which this information becomes so widely distributed and redundant in various brain regions. Obviously, an enormous amount of painstaking research on functions and interconnections between specific brain modules on the cellular level is needed to acquire this knowledge. Yet most neuroscientists agree that what is most critical to this effort is a mathematical model that could allow us to understand how the brain generates more global neuronal patterns based on interactions at the level of the synapse. If we do manage to develop such a model, much of what appears mysterious in brain function would rapidly be disclosed to scientific understanding.

Neuroscience Awaits Its Einsteins

One of the great lessons taught by physics is that the fundamental mechanisms of complex natural processes eventually yield themselves to elegant and economical mathematical descriptions. That the vast complexity of life in the universe can be viewed in terms of the interactions between quanta and field in quantum field theory is eloquent testimony to the efficacy of this assumption. Revolutions in scientific thought, which Thomas Kuhn has labeled "paradigm shifts," occur when theorists formulate testable theories that question what others in the field regard as self-evident truths. One obvious example is Einstein's idea that the classical notion of relative motion in the separate and discrete dimensions of space and time implied the prospect of an object being absolutely at rest. Questioning the validity of that assumption, he was led to doubt the existence of a hypothetical substance called the "ether" that most physicists at the time regarded as a self-evident truth.

What neuroscience is waiting for is its Einstein—or, more realistically, its Einstein along with its Bohr, Heisenberg, Schrödinger, Pauli, Dirac, and de Broglie. Scientists speculate that, as with modern physics, the first major theoretical breakthrough in neuroscience will be quickly followed by other major breakthroughs. These breakthroughs will likely take the form of theories that evince the same elegance and economy associated with other major scientific discoveries. As James Watson puts it, "I don't think consciousness will turn out to be something grand. People said that there was something grand in the cellar that gave us heredity. It turned out to be pretty simple—DNA."[13]

One research area that promises to provide insights into the global aspects of brain function is the physics of deterministic chaos, or of nonlinear systems. It is significant that the computer as research tool opened the door to this stange new world in which order and disorder exist in complementary relation. The largely accidental discovery of the physics of deterministic chaos was made in 1963 by MIT meteorologist Edward Lorenz. In order to appreciate how momentous this discovery was, it is important to understand the differences between linear and nonlinear equations. First of all, these terms refer to properties of *solutions* to equations, rather than to properties *inherent in* equations. The wave equation that describes the motion of a water wave is linear: all we need do to accurately describe the motion of a water wave is add together its different amplitudes and wavelengths. Yet most of the equations that describe phenomena in the natural world are nonlinear—adding up solutions does not lead to a new solution that accurately describes the phenomena. What has been problematic in the natural sciences is that we have been obliged to deal with most natural phenomena in terms of these mathematically intractable and almost-impossible-to-solve nonlinear equations.

While attempting to deal with the problem of long-range weather forecasting, Lorenz entered his nonlinear weather equations into a computer and waited while the computer printed out lists of the three quantities. The discovery of what would be called the physics of deterministic chaos was occasioned when Lorenz decided to stop the computer, examine the lists of numbers, enter an intermediate set for the three values, and then start the computer run again with the intermediate values functioning as initial data. This procedure seemed entirely reasonable because the individual equations were deterministic. Thus Lorenz anticipated that if the initial data, represented by the intermediate values, was the same, the computer should grind out the same solutions as before. Yet he discovered in the second computer run that not only were the values of the three quantities different from the previous run but the differences were also magnified as the run continued. What happened was that the values of the three quantities were not printed out to full machine accuracy, and this made the intermediate values used on the second run slightly different from those of the previous run. This accident proved fortuitous for science because it disclosed a property of nonlinear systems that would soon be described in terms of the physics of deterministic chaos: extreme sensitivity to initial data. What this means for weather patterns, for example, is that a gull flapping its wings off the coast of Florida could generate an infinitesimally small fluctuation in initial conditions that could, in principle, result in the chaos of a typhoon.

Although Lorenz's discovery languished for over a decade in an obscure meteorology journal, it was eventually understood that sensitivity to initial conditions plays a large role in other nonlinear systems, like the flow of water through pipes, chemical reactions, changes in wildlife populations, the flow of hormones in the human body, and the interaction of roughly 10^{14} synaptic connections in the human brain. The order that exists in such systems in complementary relation to chaos results from sensitive dependence on initial conditions, and it reveals itself in the form of attractors. An attractor can be defined as what a solution to an equation is drawn into in a computer simulation of a nonlinear system, and it can be understood by first describing the abstract notion of "state space."

The physical state of a dynamical system can be defined theoretically once we have defined all the variables for the dynamical system. A pendulum that swings back and forth on a plane can be described by just two variables: the position of the bob and its velocity. Defining the physical state of far more complicated dynamical systems, like the human brain, could require an infinite number of variables. Imagine an abstract space called a "state" or "phase" space, in which the different dimensions correspond to the number of variables describing the physical system. In the case of the pendulum, the state space is two-dimensional—one dimension represents the bob and the other the velocity. While we can easily visualize two-dimensional space, more complicated dynamical systems,

involving lots of variables and impressively large dimensions in state space, are impossible to visualize. Yet even
very complicated dynamical systems can be represented
on computer systems in terms of a single point in multidimensional state space.

Attractors can be said to "live" in state space and to
"attract" the point that is moving around in that space.
When we represent complex variables in state space, we
witness the emergence of several types of attractors. The
fixed point attractor describes a system at rest after motion has ceased. Water, swirling in a container, will eventually settle, in mathematical terms, into a fixed point
where the system is regular and predictable. An attractor
known as the *limit cycle* describes a point in phase space
that cycles around a specific closed loop; the limit cycle
attractor has been used in efforts to understand the periodic beating of the human heart. Limit cycles also have
been detected in complex chemical reactions, in which
concentrations of two chemicals oscillate back and forth.
Metabolic chemical reactions in living organisms also
oscillate in limit cycles and may explain the mechanisms
of chemical clocks in the body and the brain.

The strangest of the attractors, appropriately called the
strange attractor, can be generated only on a computer. As
the points describing the path created by the strange attractor appear on a video screen, we will see two nearby
paths emerge and then rapidly diverge. And we will also
discover that the paths created by the moving points never
return to the same location and yet always remain in a
bounded region. The result is that the paths meander
through a subspace of the whole space, creating increasingly more intricate and beautiful geometrical objects. Yet
there are no equations to describe these objects. The only
way in which we can see what they look like is to generate
them on a computer. What the bizarre behavior of the
strange attractor is revealing as it moves on the video
screen is extreme sensitivity to initial data. Any initial
difference in this data, corresponding to nearby paths in
state space, is quickly amplified.[14]

What makes these developments revolutionary is that attractors are properties of nonlinear equations, and these equations describe the real world in all of its complexity. These developments suggest that out of chaos comes order, and out of simplicity emerges complexity. Chaos has structure, and may be the probe that will allow us to detect statistical regularities in the neuronal organization of the human brain. Neuroscientists who are excited by the research possibilities provided by this probe normally point out that the interactions between neurons in the human brain more closely resemble the dynamics of a system like the weather than those of a digital computer. Receptors fluctuate rapidly under the influence of many microscopic conditions inside and outside the cell and resemble a complex chemical reaction in solution. Thus, the physics of chaos could be one of the conceptual tools that leads to major new insights into the emergent order in the seemingly chaotic system of the human brain.

Neuroscientists Walter and Alan Garfinkle have used this physics of chaos to analyze a group of neurons with cross-inhibitory coupling. Although the neurons fire erratically, there are patterns in this firing that the researchers believe can be described in terms of attractors.[15] Psychiatrist Alan King, who also holds a Ph.D. in mathematics from Cornell, used the physics of chaos to study the variables for dopamine synthesis and release. He discovered that the dopamine system appears subject to the transitions witnessed in nonlinear systems. King also has been studying panic disorder by modeling norepinephrine and its receptors in terms of nonlinear equations, and he believes he has discovered the same transitions in this unstable and supersensitive system as well.[16] Similarly, Cindy Ehlers at the Salk Institute claims to have discovered patterns in EEG studies that resemble those produced in the equations describing the nonlinear system of hydrodynamic flow.[17]

The boldest of these theorists at present is Arnold Mandell, recipient of the MacArthur Foundation Prize in 1984. Mandell has employed his understanding of nonlinear hydrodynamic systems to speculate on brain function on a more global level. Mandell's hypothesis is that the brain oscillates between two states: a laminar, or nonturbulent, state described by a fixed or periodic attractor, and a chaotic state described by the strange attractor. The same model can also describe, he suggests, the physical dynamics of the two hemispheres: the left seems to be laminar and orderly, and the right appears to be organized around a strange attractor. The more global aspect of brain function may also find its explanation, suggests Mandell, in the strange attractor. A cross section of a strange attractor shows an infinite regress of folds within folds. Since patterns associated with the strange attractor appear in computer-based studies of dopamine receptors, in the enzyme tyrosine hydroxylase, which makes dopamine, in the serotonin receptors, in single-cell neuron recordings, and in EEG patterns, these unique patterns could be inprinted, Mandell speculates, on every neuron.[18]

Prospects of Passing Turing's Test

We should not conclude from any of this that we are now on the verge of positing a theoretical model that will lead to a full scientific understanding of the more global aspects of human consciousness. Vast amounts of research will be required before we can speak of this prospect with any real conviction. The point is that there is now growing confidence among researchers in this area that we eventually will be able to map the physical substrate of human consciousness in terms of known, or potentially discoverable, scientific principles and models. Dynamic holistic models for the information storage and processing capabilities of the human brain obviously can be tested or explored only on living subjects as they interact with their environment. A window into the dynamic processes of the living brain is precisely what is being offered by new computer-based research tools like the PET scanner. A visit to any brain lab would involve becoming acquainted with other computer-based research tools, such as intracellular amplifiers, signal averagers, and voltage-controlled oscillators.

Although it seems reasonable to conclude that neuroscience will soon regard the present state of this technology as crude, the technology has, nevertheless, begun to provide information that serves as the basis for increasingly more complex theoretical models of the brain. Meanwhile, computers whose architectures are designed to emulate the organization and function of the information-processing system of the human brain—neural-net computers—are serving as research tools that allow us to incrementally disclose and model the underlying structures at work in various aspects of the brain. The resulting knowledge becomes the basis for refining and improving upon the capabilities of neural nets, or for constructing computers with other architectures. This means that if the synergistic interplay between all of these developments results in a mathematical model for global brain function, the implementation of this model on computer systems could follow shortly thereafter.

In my view, the mind that was capable of devising physical theories to describe the origins and transformations of a cosmos 15 to 20 billion years old will be able to extend knowledge of itself. As it does so, the ineffable mysteries of its own dynamics, like the once ineffable mysteries of stellar formation or subatomic particle creation, will increasingly be displaced by scientific explanation. Assuming that the knowledge acquired by neuroscience continues to be applied by cognitive scientists as models for the more mindlike computer, it is reasonable to predict that a computer capable of passing the Turing test, and of rather quickly evolving into an intelligence superior to our own, is a very realistic prospect.

Building a computer with these capabilites will require knowledge that we do not yet have and computer designs, based on related components, that do not yet exist. Those of us who would prefer to believe that the creation of such

a computer will never happen should perhaps remind ourselves of the following: (1) the study of the human brain on
a level that can properly be called scientific has only recently begun; (2) understanding of basic principles of nature in areas such as quantum field theory and the physics
of deterministic chaos is also fairly recent; and (3) computer science is still in its infancy. When we contemplate
the progress that will be made in all of these related fields
in the foreseeable future, individually and synergistically,
the reasonable conclusion is that we will eventually see a
computer pass the Turing test.

Most of the systematic attempts that have been made
thus far to undermine the AI evolution-of-consciousness
hypothesis have sought to demonstrate that a computer
can never pass the the Turing test or will never be able to
meet a reasonably complete set of performance criteria for
what constitutes a conscious system. For reasons we will
explore in some detail later, these arguments have not
proven persuasive for the advocates of the hypothesis. If
we are to convincingly undermine or refute the hypothesis
in ways that are persuasive to its advocates, we must, in
my view, be able to demonstrate the following within the
context of scientific knowledge: (1) the evolution of a conscious computer is not mandated by the lawful regularities
of natural evolution; and (2) an AI computer system
deemed conscious by the Turing criteria cannot "in principle" be presumed conscious as we are conscious. As I
hope to demonstrate in the last two chapters, a close reading of the present state of scientific knowledge in both
biology and physics allows us to provide substantive validity for both of these assertions.

Yet undermining the scientific legitimations of the AI
evolution-of-consciousness hypothesis, as I noted earlier, is
only a small part of the challenge for those of us committed to nurturing and protecting the ultimate value of human life and consciousness in the technological future.
When a computer passes the Turing test, the questions of
what constitutes self, human consciousness, or human

nature will no longer be relegated primarily to sophomore classes in philosophy or religion. As the cognitive scientist Michael Arbib puts it, "Now perhaps it is not presumptuous to warn ourselves that the concurrent emergence of computer technology and cognitive science requires an immense effort of the philosophical imagination if it is not to lead to yet another massive tragedy in human experience."[19] One early indication that we had best begin to rigorously exercise our philosophical—and moral—imaginations in order to avoid another massive tragedy in human affairs is that we are already in the process of allowing computer systems to displace human decision making in a number of important areas.

CHAPTER 3

The Minds We Make: The Present Generation of Computers

The robots will take many forms: work cells of disembodied arms, roving material-handling small carts, or multiarmed "jack of all trade machines" that can be moved to a new work area, equipped with a new set of tools, reprogrammed and put to work. . . . The small army of sophisticated machines will be supervised by a machine as well—the centralized factory computers. In a sense, the factory will be one enormous robot, the computer its guiding intelligence, and the machines on the floor part of the grand design.
                                                —Arthur C. Clarke
                                                 July 20, 1919

What might be called "AI bashing" has recently become fashionable in the debate over the future of computer technologies. Those engaged in this practice generally argue that the effort over the past thirty years to create a computer system that can simulate human faculties like creativity, judgment, and intuition has failed miserably. According to these critics, those who have taken seriously the claims of AI researchers that such a computer system could exist have failed to appreciate that everything a computer does is based on the 0/1 notation of binary numbers, and the off/on channels of electrical transistors. In order to put the exaggerated claims of AI experts in perspective, the critics suggest that we need only appreciate the fact that any computer program, no matter how impressive, reduces logically to extremely simple relationships expressed in words such as *and, or, both, neither,* and *implies.* On the most basic level, the critics remind us, the computer is nothing more than effective procedures or programs based on binary arithmetic and the flow of electrons in semiconductors. Since this mathematical logic is not capable of dealing with the complexity of ordinary problems routinely solved by the human brain, the usual conclusion of these arguments is that the computer can never, in principle, emulate the ability of the human brain to deal with such problems. The AI bashers have also received considerable help in winning converts to their position by the tendency of developers of AI systems and those who write about these systems in the popular press to exaggerate the extent to which these systems can emulate human brain function.

Yet the authors of the "what computers cannot do" arguments are rarely computer scientists. Even those computer scientists who are outspoken critics of the AI evolution-of-consciousness hypothesis tend not to place any upper limits on the capabilities of computers, or to argue that the computer can never "in principle" emulate complex functions of the human mind. Yet the critics are correct on one point: "conventional" computers cannot "in principle" fully emulate the manner in which the human brain processes information. The intelligence of contemporary AI systems is clearly that of computer scientists creating complex programs. However, conventional AI computers are being displaced by new generations of such computers whose principles of organization *are* modeled, however crudely at this point, after those of the human brain. When we look at the capabilities of the present generation of conventional computer technologies, and contemplate the capabilities of the coming generations of AI computers built on neural-net architectures, the "what computers cannot do" arguments seem as ill-advised as the claims of some AI experts that a conscious computer is just around the corner.

Robotics and the Human Sensorium

If a computer deemed conscious by the Turing criteria is to exist on a physical substate other than the human brain, it must at some stage develop complex feedback mechanisms for interacting with and learning from its environment. It must, in other words, develop the rough equivalent of the human sensorium. The research area where this problem is addressed most directly is robotics. If we compare the abilities of the current generation of robots to even the most primitive of biological systems, we may not be terribly impressed. As the robotics expert Hans Moravec of Carnegie-Mellon University puts it, "present robot systems are now similar in power to the control systems of insects."[1] On the other hand, the control system of insects was the product of billions of years of Darwinian evolution, whereas the evolution of modern robotics systems has only just begun. Professor Ichiro Kata of Japan has claimed that his robot system, which has an intelligent upper torso and can read music and play the organ, has an intelligence approximately that of a five-year-old.[2] Although neuroscientists would undoubtedly view this claim as utter nonsense, the fact remains that we have made rapid progress in this area in little time (see Figure 9).

We have known for some years how to design and program a robotics system that executes a series of fixed or preprogrammed movements, like arms that do spot welding on automobile assembly lines. The next challenge is to create robotics systems that fully emulate the ability of human limbs—particularly the human hand—to manipulate objects in three-dimensional space, and that function based on sensory information analogous to human sight and touch. More than a hundred companies market industrial computer vision systems and devices, and the market for these systems is growing at a factor of four every year.[3] Most of these systems are designed to inspect products like circuit boards or precision-machined parts for defects, in environments where light is controlled and uniform.

Figure 9

Odex climbing stairs.

The objects they inspect typically have well-known and defined shapes with high-contrast edges, and the methodology used is simple template matching. In other words, the robot compares the observed outlines of the object with a model of the object in its computer memory. The other major industrial use of these systems involves assembly-line robots, when there is a need to adjust the preprogrammed movement of a robotic arm so that it is precisely aligned with the contours of the object to be manipulated.

The technology used in robotic arms with limited vision systems is fairly straightforward. A simple pattern of light, like an array of stripes, falls across the surface of an object in a pattern of curves that outlines the surface. Using simple geometry, the vision system traces the stripes and derives the three-dimensional shape of the object by comparing the observed shape with the shapes programmed in memory. Although this methodology works well when the pattern of shapes is limited and where the light can be controlled, it is not suitable for manipulating randomly oriented objects where lighting is hard to control—such as a situation where machine parts are scattered on a floor or jumbled in a bin.

Berthold Horn and his colleagues at MIT have developed a promising new approach to solving these problems. Their basic idea is to illuminate the pile of parts from three separate directions, thus giving the computer three separate images to work with. This approach allows each point of the surface of a given part to be illuminated differently in the three images, or to have three different brightness values. The computer observes these values and uses them to calculate the orientation of each point of surface. After the computer constructs a pattern of surface images for the whole image, it compares the pattern it "sees" with the patterns associated with each object. This methodology allows a robot to identify individual objects in terms of their precise location in the defined space, and to move or manipulate them more precisely and quickly than a human worker.[4]

Yet simple template matching and special lighting tricks will not allow a computer to emulate human vision, which is capable of recognizing complex objects in three-dimensional space where there is no way of knowing beforehand what objects will be found. In contrast with the human eye, however, artificial vision systems are not restricted to visible light and do not need to passively wait until the radiation impacts them. Radar, for example, can probe a scene at night and form the basis for an active vision system. Since radar is capable of measuring the distance to every point of every object in its field, it greatly simplifies the problem of working in three dimensions. Many of these same advantages are offered by sonar systems using ultrasound, or laser ranging systems using laser impulses. Tomasso Poggio and his colleagues at MIT are now exploring regularization techniques of mathematical physics that could provide a way of putting a variety of different robotic eyes or vision modules into a common mathematical framework.[5]

The largest problem in developing better robotic vision systems is deriving an improved theoretical model for how image processing occurs in the human brain. Researchers worldwide are exploring multistage vision processing systems like that employed by the human brain, and the ultra-high-speed computational power these systems will require could be available in the sixth generation of computer technologies. But since the eyes required by robots are task-specific, new applications for "seeing" robots will not have to wait until multistage vision processing systems have been developed. The experimental model of a weed-killing robot being developed at Purdue University, for example, relies on infrared sensors to target those plants that will be sprayed with weed killer. A University of California at Davis robot uses x-ray sensors to gauge the plumpness and density of a lettuce plant to determine if it is ripe for picking; this robot performed better in one test than experienced human lettuce pickers. And robots used in the nuclear industry "see" radiation leaks with gamma radiation sensors.

Similarly, robots are being equipped with a cybernetic epidermis, or a complex array of force sensors analogous to those in the human skin. A system at MIT uses three layers, with the middle layer consisting of a set of electrical conductors and the outer layers of a flexible synthetic hide. Variations on this design include the system at Carnegie-Mellon, which employs pressure-sensitive dots of polymer that produce an electrical signal when squeezed; a system at the University of Florida that consists of a rubber skin with a rigid pattern that vibrates under pressure; and one at Stanford University that features electronic hairs inside a robot glove that read varying pressures on the glove.

Progress has also been made in improving the dexterity of robotic arms equipped with various vision systems. AT&T's Bell Laboratories in New Jersey has a robot that plays a serviceable, mainly defensive game of Ping-Pong. The intent of such inventions is to solve some of the problems involved in robotic manipulation of objects in three-dimensional space in real time. The so-called Stanford Jet Propulsion Laboratory hand can pick up wine glasses with its individually coordinated fingers. Similarly, the Utah-MIT hand can grasp an egg, crack it, dump its contents into a bowl, and then beat it at high speed with its index finger. Although these tasks may seem trivial when a human being does them, developing robots that can do them is a formidable task. The Ping-Pong player at Bell Labs, for example, relies on an array of four television cameras and ten processors of different kinds, and it calculates the spin of the ball in the fourth dimension (see Figures 10 and 11).

At the moment a wide range of automatic systems incorporating robotics, control systems, and artificial intelligence are employed in advanced production systems and defense products. When robots with improved vision and touch capabilities are linked to and directed by expert systems that monitor all the complex variables of a factory or power plant, we could create the first "completely" automated production system. The AI systems in the fully automated production systems of the future will be able to diagnose problems, direct the robot to make the necessary repairs, and, in general, keep the production system supplied and running with minimal disruption. Existing examples of such production systems are the Fujitsu Fanuc factory, where a hundred robots and sixty workers produce ten thousand electric motors monthly, and the Magnesans Corporation's factory in southern Sweden, where robots haul parts to work areas at an inhuman pace and under inhumane conditions. In the Swedish production system, on-the-spot monitoring occurs on the weekends, and the nearest human manager is typically ten miles away.

Figure 10

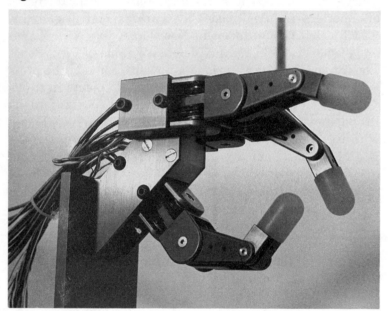

MIT Salisbury hand.

Evolution and the Feeling Computer

Since computer systems tend to be integrated, we can anticipate more linkage between complex AI "central" computers and their robotic extensions. The effect will be

Figure 11

Robot hand developed by GMFanuc.

to provide advanced computer systems with their own version of an extended sensorium, thus allowing continual feedback of stimuli in a complex, changing environment. In terms of the AI evolution-of-consciousness hypothesis, the ability of AI systems to learn in a complex environment represents an essential phase in the evolution of the conscious computer. As Moravec puts it in "Robots That Rove," "Organisms and mechanisms do not exist in isolation, but are systems with their environments, and those on the prowl in general have a richer environment than those rooted in one place. I believe the same pressures are at work in the technological evolution of robots, and, by that analogy, mobile robots are the most likely route to solutions of some of the most vexing problems on the way to true artificial intelligence—problems such as how to program common-sense reasoning and learning from sensory experience." Just as Darwinian evolution taught animals emotions like caution and fear, movement within a changing environment will, concludes Moravec, do the same for robots.[6] Moravec's underlying assumption is that the computer is a form of intelligence capable of evolving into higher forms of intelligence as a result of its own experience. The computer will, he suggests, evolve means of evaluating and responding to complex environmental stimuli in its own quest for survival.

Marvin Minsky is another cognitive scientist who has theorized about how "emotion" can be simulated in the emergent consciousness of computer technologies. His thesis is that emotions focus our attention in accordance with goals and motives that are biologically relevant, or that have become consistent with our own cognitive styles or global programs. Since productive thinking involves the use of analogy and metaphor, which are often false and misleading, emotion also functions as part of the mechanism that allows the mind to suppress or ignore inappropriate comparisons. In other words, "bugs" in the wet machine, like ineffective or destructive thought processes, are suppressed or eliminated by emotion. Since emotions, as we saw earlier, seem to operate in the human brain in terms of two states, agreeable or disagreeable, the two-state character of emotions would also be an essential design feature of a computer that could emulate human emotions. Also, since the physiological responses to primal emotions, such as fear, anger, or joy, are identical, they do not themselves, concludes Minksy, direct the mind. It is rather, he argues, mind that directs emotion, or that invokes the changes in blood pressure, breathing, heart rate, adrenaline level, etc., that we associate with emotion.

Minsky concludes, therefore, that the equivalent of emotion in the intelligent computer would be global directives that force attention on some aspect of the computer's experience, or that block or suppress certain thoughts and impulses. If Minsky's thesis is correct, the rough equivalent of emotions in an AI system capable of associative reasoning could be programmed in as global directives or could emerge as a consequence of experience.[7] As he recently summarized the situation, in the last decade "neurologists have increasingly come to believe that the powers of the human mind emerge not from some central neural magic, but from a host of prosaic parts and a load of common sense."[8]

In the case of the human brain, survival responses with emotional coloration evolved before the higher-level executive schemas associated with the cerebral cortex. But the reverse will be true in the evolution of computer intelligence: the higher-level executive schemas associated with the AI application of the system will come first. It is, therefore, those higher-level schemas that will govern the development of commonsense reasoning and learning from sensory experience in the emergent conscious computer. If we consider the human emotions that the higher-level executive schemas might serve as goal orientations in advanced AI systems of the future, this last observation could be more than the subject of idle intellectual curiosity.

Computer companies, for example, have produced for the Pentagon a number of expert systems that run war games, or computerized simulations of battles. TRW Defense Systems of California has been developing an artificial intelligence system that emulates the collective wisdom of generals playing war games.[9] Computer systems featuring computerized modeling techniques from the social sciences have also been developed for use in the so-called crisis management area. For example, during the Vietnam War, prototypes of such systems reportedly helped planners select "hostile" villages as bombing targets based on a set of parameters. More recently, the orchestration of the 1983 Grenada invasion was based in part on models provided by expert systems used by the Crisis Management and Planning Group within the National Security Council. This system is apparently capable of generating information in a "composite video form" using "state-of-the-art graphics," and thereby models an international crisis in ways that can more easily lead to effective action.[10] The Joint Chiefs of Staff have access to their own expert modeling and simulating system called FORECASTS, which went on-line in 1984. This system uses "country-specific information" to project probable futures for some 130 nations over a period of twenty or thirty years. The database for each country includes over a thousand key indicators, and most correlate with a time series of values. This effort to simulate the interplay between variables over time presumably provides planners with a more circumspect view of the risks and rewards of undertaking military action in the present. A database management system also allows the FORECASTS system to be queried and updated.[11]

Computer as Dedicated Expert

AI bashers, as we noted, have received considerable assistance in advancing their "what computers cannot do" arguments by the tendency of developers of AI systems— or more often those who describe these systems in the popular press—to exaggerate the mindlike capabilities of these systems. One of the early examples of this kind of exaggeration appeared in press releases describing the abilities of an AI program developed by Herbert Simon and Allen Newell at Dartmouth College in 1956. Known as the Logic Theorist, the program was designed to take logical propositions and prove them point by point. The unexpected result was that the program devised a proof that two human mathematical geniuses, Bertrand Russell and Alfred North Whitehead, had missed in their monumental *Principia Mathematica*.

As the story was told in the popular press, what was most remarkable about ,this feat was that the proof of the Whitehead-Russell theorem was not "predictable," and the programmers could not anticipate what the program would do under a given set of conditions. Since this is a prime criterion of human intelligence, the new program was widely heralded as displaying one aspect of this complex process. However, anyone who was familiar with the design of the program could see that comparing its mathematical abilities with those of human mathematical geniuses was nothing short of absurd. That Russell and Whitehead should have missed one of the shortest proofs in the process of constructing thousands of proofs is, first of all, understandable. More important, the Logic Theorist did not turn up this missing proof as a result of mathematical intuition or creativity. All it displayed was the ability of a sophisticated computer program to crunch numbers in a rigorous logical sequence. Although some programs have been developed since 1956 that have provided original results of mathematical interest, the Logic Theorist was merely a rudimentary effort of this kind.

Yet if reliable results for a task demand can be arrived at through rules and procedures translatable into monotonic computer logic, AI systems, particularly when we factor in the anticipated thousandfold increase in speed and computing power of the next or fifth generation of computers, could become far better at such tasks than a human intelligence. Internist-1, for example, is an expert system that makes diagnoses in internal medicine. It is one in a series of expert systems developed in the Caduceus Project at the University of Pittsburgh. The results of a competition between the diagnostic ability of Internist-1 and human experts were recently published in *The New England Journal of Medicine*. Internist-1 misdiagnosed 18 out of a total of 43 cases, while the human physicians at Massachusetts General Hospital misdiagnosed 15 of these cases. A panel of doctors who discussed each case did somewhat better, with only 8 instances of misdiagnosis.[12]

The explanation that we might prefer to account for this difference is that the human intelligence is possessed of something called "intuition," which a computer cannot emulate. A more reasonable explanation is that intuition in this type of situation is rule-based, and we have not yet created an AI diagnostic system for internal medicine that knows all the rules. Although a physician may have a holistic understanding of the patient that the computer cannot manage, conclusions in medical diagnoses do tend to follow monotonic reasoning or rules. This means that a system like Internist-1 could prove itself more capable of making accurate diagnoses than any single human intelligence in the next generation or so of this technology. Such a system could learn and apply rules gained from the experience of numerous human experts in numerous situations. Wherever rule-based procedures coincide with the manner in which a human intelligence arrives at a best-case solution to any complex problem, we are likely over time to find expert systems providing the solutions. This should be the case even if an optimum choice cannot be made by an expert system through exhaustive search or rigorous calculation. In this situation, AI programmers have typically appealed to heuristics, or a kind of rule-of-thumb approach, leading to a best-case approximation.

If we do not understand the internal workings of such systems, it is quite easy to presume that they are more mindlike than is actually the case. For another example, take the manner in which an expert system named Bacon—in honor of Francis Bacon—was described in the popular press shortly after it was developed in the 1970s. This system, we were told, deduced laws of nature based on scientific facts and independently discovered a law of planetary motion. Equally remarkable, according to the press releases, Bacon analyzed scientific facts pertaining to chemical elements and deduced on its own a key law in this area as well. Here again, if one understood the design of the program, the suggestion that Bacon could discover laws of nature in the manner of a human scientist would immediately be recognized as unadulterated hype. What

Bacon was capable of was a fancy version of curve fitting, and of deducing formulae that subsume a collection of data points. A similar account in the popular press touted the capabilities of Automated Mathematician, a system invented in 1976 by Douglas Lenat at Stanford University. It was designed to deal with if-then rules and concepts, such as equality, sets, and addition. According to the press releases, Automated Mathematician had moved within hours from grade school arithmetic to college mathematics and had even managed to deduce some 200 theories about numbers, including the idea that some numbers are prime. Although Automated Mathematician was an interesting and innovative program, it could not manage even grade-school arithmetic, much less college-level mathematics.

More recently, Lenat has committed himself to developing a system capable of explanation-based learning, known as Cyc for "encyclopedia." Explanation-based learning involves developing a computer system that can "observe" objects and phenomena and determine on its own how they work. The intent in the Cyc system is to provide the computer with as much as possible of "what every child knows." Lenat trains his database by selecting random newspaper and encyclopedia entries and then provides the computer with everything it needs to "know" to comprehend a given idea. For example, if a sentence reads "The man was drinking from a cup," the computer needs to understand the size, purpose, and function of a typical cup, including the notion that the open end must point up to prevent the liquid from flowing out. The computer also needs to know, in a crude sense at least, something about what a man is, what function drinking serves, and, in short, to comprehend the situation without any feedback from the programmer. Marvin Minsky was recently quoted in an article in *Discover* magazine as saying that a computer containing everyday information of this sort would require a few million entries. If Cyc-type programs are perfected, and if 16 million bit chips are available in three or four years at a cost of roughly $15 each, then, according to Minsky, the use of three such chips could allow such programs to be made available on personal computers for a cost of only a few hundred dollars.[13] The more realistic interpretation of this situation is that we have no idea how to encode most commonsense knowledge, and that the estimate of a few million entries is pure guesswork.

When the AI bashers assert that expert systems are merely "idiot savants" dealing only with facts supplied by programmers, they are at the moment correct. Yet all indications are that AI systems capable of functioning as autonomous learners and complex problem solvers will be operational very soon. If progress in explanation-based learning continues to be as rapid as many experts in the field now anticipate it will be, we can expect an exponential increase in the use of expert systems over the next twenty years. The revolution in expert systems is likely to present us with a number of disturbing prospects, ranging from the impact on human managers in the workplace to a terrible sense of powerlessness in understanding, or controlling, those aspects of everyday reality that are managed by computer systems.

Given that human beings are reluctant to make large decisions within complex social organizations, allowing computer systems to take the lead has psychological appeal. The computer does not "care" whether it makes a mistake, and the responsibility for those mistakes can be rather conveniently passed off to those who program and manage computer systems. Where the computer is most likely to err is in dealing with situational factors that are not easily represented in a series of rules or if-then statements. These factors are particularly difficult to manage and represent in social science applications, where learned or culturally derived ideological commitments and beliefs come into play.

Mind-Machines in Social Science Applications

One of the early applications in social science, called POLITICS, was developed by a group headed by Roger

Schank, Director of the Yale Artificial Intelligence Program. Here again media hype exaggerated the capabilities of a system that never got beyond the mock-up stage of development. Schank and his team began with the assumption that human beings make ideological decisions in terms of "scripts." They also assumed that scripts connect pieces of information into "stories" that describe new and unexpected situations. In order to build scripts, the computer must work with information about how human beings achieve goals with plans, or series of projected actions. According to the popular press, POLITICS built its scripts on the basis of ideological theories about national and international motivation, and incorporated them into stories in its internal memory in such a way that it could answer questions, make predictions about future events, and speculate on how the United States might respond in a particular instance. In truth, POLITICS could not generate any conversation other than in the three or four reported examples, and we are nowhere near building a program that can converse about politics in this fashion.

If one does not know these facts, then a printout of this mock-up system's responses to political questions based on particular ideological scripts could give the impression that the system is capable of providing a rather sophisticated analysis of possible responses to a complex political situation. Presuming that the script emulates a right-wing ideology in considering the consequences of a Russian invasion of Czechoslovakia, a typical printout would read as follows:

> *Q:* Why did Russia mass troups on the Czech border?
> *A:* Because Russia thought it could take political control of Czechoslovakia by sending in troops.
> *Q:* What will Russia do next?
> *A:* Russia will tell its troops to start the invasion.
> *Q:* What else will Russia do?
> *A:* Russia will wait for Czechoslovakia to give in to Russian demands.

Q: What happens if Czechoslovakia does not give in?
A: Russia may decide to start the invasion.
Q: What should the United States do?
A: The United States should intervene militarily.
Q: What else could the United States do?
A: The United States can do nothing, or it can intervene diplomatically by conferring with Russia about Czechoslovakia. These alternatives are bad for the United States.

In fairness to the developers of this system, a liberal or left-wing script would result in a set of quite different responses.

Although many systems like POLITICS have been funded by the Pentagon's Defense Advanced Research Project (DARPA), there is no indication that such systems have provided input that served as the sole basis for any decisions made in international politics. There are, however, many instances in which AI computers have influenced decisions, and all indications are that this trend will continue. What is troublesome is that the users of increasingly more complex AI systems are often unaware of the internal design and limitations of these systems, and are easily enticed into presuming that the analysis is more detailed, complex, and "reasoned" than is actually the case.

Take, for example, a more recent example of an AI system called SIGMA, which is purportedly designed to predict and model future events. Developed by the Policy Analysis Company, SIGMA translates a confusing array of future possibilities into percentage probabilities that an event will occur. SIGMA is based on an understanding of probabilities from quantum physics, and it infers what might happen with an element of indeterminacy. Although one future scenario may not be interesting in and of itself, a group of scenarios from SIGMA is alleged to be useful in forecasting and strategic planning. Since the probabilities used by the system include events which more conventional forecasting systems would not include because the odds against them happening are too great, the unlikely, although possible, event can be projected and its consequences evaluated.

In one recent and unclassified test of SIGMA at the Department of Defense's Industrial College of the Armed Forces, fourteen participants nominated and evaluated thirty-three future events considered important to the security of the United States over the next twenty years. In response to this input, SIGMA generated fourteen unique scenarios for the future. The first two of the scenarios forecast separately the following events: June 1991—molecular chip developed; June 1992—drugs developed to enhance brain function; July 1993—anti-aging drug developed; and January 1998—brain dump to computer is developed (see Figure 12). If one knows anything about quantum indeterminacy, it is easy to conclude that SIGMA is no more useful in forecasting future events than the astrology column in your local newspaper. Quantum indeterminacy, even though it prescribes certain limits to the range of probable outcomes in making measurements or observations of subatomic events, is nevertheless random, and therefore indeterminate. That the predictions of SIGMA appear to have been taken rather seriously by those who studied them in the Industrial College of the Armed Forces is itself testimony to the fact that AI systems for social science applications could be far more dangerous in the technological future than we have yet to fully comprehend.

Obviously AI systems should be used responsibly, which means in part recognizing their limitations by understanding their internal design and capabilities. Yet interacting with an "intelligent" AI system can easily entice one into feeling that one is dealing with a mindlike intelligence. The classic example of a computer program that can create this illusion, based on fairly simple programming techniques, was developed in the 1970s by Joseph Weizenbaum. The ELIZA system was programmed to make responses in English that emulate responses that

Figure 12   National Security

Scenario 1

This is what happens:

May 1987	Terrorists detonate biochemical bomb
Sep 1989	U.S.S.R. becomes net energy importer
Nov 1989	AIDS is found to be spread by mosquitoes
Jan 1990	Childless households increase from 48% to 75%
May 1991	Robot infantrymen are deployed
Jun 1992	Drugs developed to enchance the brain
Apr 1993	U.S. pulls out of Korea
Jan 1994	Learning information network communications
Jan 1994	Earthquake prediction capability is perfected
May 1994	Biochemical warfare in Iraq/Iran war
Dec 1994	New "earth" found at nearby star
Jan 1996	Brain dump to computer developed
May 1999	Used human parts are reconstituted
Jan 2000	Commission on ethics established
May 2000	Foreign business intelligence center founded
Apr 2001	"Red Tide" devastates Latin economies
Jul 2002	Early warning systems sabotaged
Feb 2003	U.S. no longer number one in farm production
Apr 2006	Global recession

This is what does NOT happen:

Engineer/scientist shortage
Polymer-matrix composite materials developed
Mental telepathy validated
Anti-aging drug developed
Brain exams forecast job performance
High unemployment due to no retirement
U.S. pulls out of NATO
Contact with extraterrestrials
Pacific nuclear-free zone
Molecular chip developed
Fission is number-one energy source
Nonnuclear metals memory developed
No restriction on servicewomen
Higher standards in high schools are met

Scenario 2

This is what happens:

May 1987 U.S.S.R. becomes net energy importer
May 1988 U.S. pulls out of Korea
Oct 1990 Commission on ethics established
Nov 1990 Higher standards in high schools are met
Jun 1991 Molecular chip developed
Oct 1991 U.S. no longer number one in farm production
Jul 1993 Anti-aging drug developed
May 1994 Earthquake prediction capability is perfected
Aug 1994 Fission is number-one energy source
Nov 1994 Learning information network communications
Jan 1996 AIDS is found to be spread by mosquitoes
Feb 1996 Childless households increase from 48% to 75%
Oct 1999 NO restriction on servicewomen
May 2001 Brain dump to computer developed
Sep 2004 Terrorists detonate biochemical bomb
Mar 2005 Robot infantrymen are deployed

This is what does NOT happen:
Engineer/scientist shortage
Polymer-matrix composite materials developed
Mental telepathy validated
Drugs developed to enhance the brain
Foreign business intelligence center founded
Brain exams forcast job performance
High unemployment due to no retirement
"Red Tide" devastates Latin economies
Early warning systems sabotaged
U.S. pulls out of NATO
Contact with extraterrestrials
New "earth" found at nearby star
Pacific nuclear-free zone
Nonnuclear metals memory developed
Used human parts are reconstituted
Global recession
Biochemical warfare in Iraq/Iran war

Two alternative scenarios for U.S. national security, based on thirty-three possible events. SIGMA "rolled the dice" for the events, using probabilites determined by workshop participants, and came up with differing versions of what will or will not occur over the next twenty years.   © 1986 The Policy Analysis Co., Inc.

might be made by a psychotherapist. Here is a typical
exchange between human patient and computer program:

Patient: Men are all alike.
Computer: In what way?
Patient: They're always bugging us about something
or other.
Computer: Can you think of a specific example?
Patient: Well, my boyfriend made me come here.
Computer: Your boyfriend made you come here?
Patient: He says I'm depressed much of the time.
Computer: I am sorry to hear you are depressed.
Patient: It's true. I am unhappy.
Computer: Do you think coming here will help you
not be unhappy?
Patient: I need some help. That much seems certain.
Computer: What would it mean to you to get some
help?
Patient: Perhaps I can learn to get along with my
mother.
Computer: Tell me more about your family.
Patient: My mother takes care of me.
Computer: Who else in your family takes care of you?
Patient: My father.
Computer: Your father?
Patient: You are like my father in some ways.
Computer: What resemblance do you see?
Patient: You are not very aggressive, but I think you
don't want me to notice that.
Computer: What makes you think I am not very ag-
gressive?
Patient: You don't argue with me.
Computer: Why do you think I don't argue with you?
Patient: You are afraid of me.
Computer: Does it please you to think I am afraid of
you?
Patient: My father is afraid of everybody.
Computer: What else comes to your mind when you
think of your father?
Patient: Bullies.

Computer: Does this have anything to do with the
fact that your boyfriend made you come here?

If we did not understand ELIZA's program, we might
conclude that this machine could pass the Turing test.
Even some of Weizenbaum's computer-literate students
and colleagues came to relate to ELIZA as if it were a
person capable of "human" understanding. ELIZA did
not, of course, understand either the question or the response, and was merely running a program based primarily on grammatical substitution. It was programmed, for
example, to substitute *you* for *I*, *are* for *am*, and then to
add as a prefix a list of stock phrases used in so-called
mirroring techniques in therapy, like "I understand
that . . ." or "Are you telling me that . . ." Thus the statement "I am happy" will be analyzed as "I am" plus X, and
ELIZA will transform "I am" into "You are," add a prefix
such as "Why do you tell me that . . ." and respond "Why
do you tell me that you are happy?"[14]

The fact that intelligent and computer-literate people
were easily enticed into believing that ELIZA displayed a
mindlike intelligence, and often showed disappointment
when they led the computer to predictable or meaningless
responses, is made more interesting by the fact that this
was in computer terms a "dumb" program. The AI systems that we are now producing are not dumb in this
sense, and AI systems now under development on neural
nets, if the developers of these systems are correct, will
soon be considerably less addled than ELIZA. And we also
must not ignore the fact that considerable progress has
been made in social science applications of AI systems on
conventional computers, in an effort to model the impacts
of belief systems, goal hierarchies, and personality traits.

Walt Sylvan and his colleagues at Syracuse University,
for example, have developed the "Walt Rostow Machine,"
which is designed to read diplomatic cables that were sent
by U.S. officials in Saigon during the 1960s. The system

produces "policy memos" recommending courses of action, and these memos are compared with the actual memos written by Rostow. Similarly, Stuart Thorson, also at Syracuse, has developed computer models based on heuristic reasoning techniques that identify, based on the data available at the time, the factors that led President Kennedy and others to the Cuban Missile Crisis. And Howard Aiker and his colleagues at MIT have designed an AI system to work out the underlying logic of political debates, based on the assumption that the seemingly irrational elements in such debates disclose an underlying logic of discourse.[15] This research is in its nascent stage, and none of these systems are as sophisticated as the press reports make them out to be. Yet considerable progress is being made in this area, and regardless of the limitations inherent in the design of these systems, they are increasingly being used as tools for decision making and policy planning by individuals with the power to shape political, social, and economic reality.

When AI systems in social science applications are equipped with a natural language interface, or the ability to read and respond to normal written or spoken sentences, the human tendency to anthropomorphize could be greatly magnified. And that could augment the more dangerous tendency to allow the AI system to make decisions and manage other systems, even when those tasks might be better performed by human intelligence. This problem is greatly amplified when we consider the development history and subsequent use of theory-based systems like those used for crisis management and social science applications. In the development stage, as Weizenbaum explains, such systems resemble patchworks put together by teams of programmers over several years. Since the original programmers tend to turn their attention to other pursuits following the development stage, these gigantic systems are often used by those who do not understand their inner workings. According to Weizenbaum, the consequences tend to be "first that decisions are made on the basis of rules and criteria no one knows explicitly, and second that the system of rules and criteria become immune to change."[16]

New Architectures for AI Systems

Although we have demonstrated considerable ingenuity in developing AI systems on conventional computer architecture, the range of applications for these systems has been circumscribed by programming constraints imposed by the architecture itself. Enormous progress obviously has been made in developing new central processing units and memory and input-output devices. Yet the design of the computer itself has not changed significantly since ENIAC went to work in 1946. We are now in the process, however, of developing a new generation of computer systems based on architectures modeled after the internal organization and function of the human brain. When we consider the new possibilities these alternate architectures present for developing AI systems in crisis management, social science applications, and for general problem solving and decision making in virtually any domain of human life, those who champion the "what computers cannot do" position could become victims of future shock. Since these new systems are in only a nascent stage of development, one cannot assume that the technological possibilities as they are conceived by the planners and developers will quickly become realities. Yet those of us concerned about the technological future had better become familiar with these possibilities and take a little comfort in the fact that some of the claims are, at the moment at least, overblown and exaggerated.

One example of a new computer design modeled in part after the human brain is the Connection Machine. Invented at the MIT Artificial Intelligence Laboratory, this system has been developed by a Cambridge-based company called Thinking Machines. The 65,536 fine-grained processors in the Connection Machine are roughly analogous in concept, if not in size, to the brain's network of neuronal processing units. First, the processors are arranged on a grid so that each communicates with its neighbor on four sides. Second, the so-called "broadcast network," or slower communication line, passes through all the processors and links each to a central computer. Finally, a "16-dimensional-hypercube network" allows connections between this formidable number of processors; each can communicate with the other by sending a signal through four communications lines. The alternative of connecting each processor to every other processor would result in a formidable wiring task involving more than two billion wires.

The Connection Machine breaks up large problems into smaller, more manageable chunks, and then parcels them out to separate areas of its processing network. In the effort to understand how the Earth shifts in a quake, for example, the computer models the terrain and then simulates how the various processes would unfold. For sheer number crunching, other computers, like the Cray, are preferred. But the Connection Machine is ideal for dealing with large problems with many loose ends, like image processing and graphics. Equally important, the system is capable of "learning" and can improve its performance with successive trials. Another application contemplated for the Connection Machine is as a two-dimensional retina that could recognize lines or edges when adjacent processors register a common light value along a given direction. After identifying these lines and edges, the multiprocessor system could use them to build an abstract, higher-level model of what the retina sees. This process would emulate the manner in which the sensory data in the human eye is translated into higher-level codes during progressive stages of the vision process.

The design breakthrough that makes all of this conceivable allows connections between large numbers of processors in some closer approximation to the number of interconnected neurons in the human brain. Multiprocessor computers, like the Connection Machine, will help solve large problems in high-energy physics, aerospace engineering, and computer-aided design of products like computer chips and airplanes. Research groups in fifty universities, and numerous other groups in industrial laboratories and start-up companies around the world, are experimenting with designs that will result in a massive quantitative increase in computing power. Since such power tends to correlate positively with increased computer intelligence, we may be moving toward the creation of computers with formidable skills.

CHAPTER 4

The Neural-Network Revolution: Modeling the Emergent Mind

Mind, n.—A mysterious form of matter secreted by the brain. Its chief activity consists of the endeavor to ascertain its own nature, the futility of the attempt being due to the fact that it has nothing but itself to know itself with.
—Ambrose Bierce
The Devil's Dictionary

John Lambe, a solid-state physicist at NASA's Jet Propulsion Laboratory in Pasadena, California, was among the first to translate recent mathematical theory on neural networks into practice. The board of Lambe's prototype is laid out on a chunk of wood roughly the size of a chessboard, and the maze of wires, switches, and other electronic components resembles a teenage hobbyist's attempt to build a computer from parts pirated from abandoned systems. Yet the switches on this board can turn on and off in a manner that programs various "memories" into the network. If the network is presented with a new input pattern, a stored memory that most closely resembles this pattern will be retrieved by the circuits. What the humble appearance of this system disguises is a radical departure

101

in the design of computer systems, a shift from the long-held belief that human thought can be represented solely in terms of a system of symbols represented by logical rules. Thinking as modeled in Lambe's computer is an intuitive, pattern-matching, prone-to-mistakes activity in which rule and symbol processing is an emergent activity. The higher-level and overt functions we tend to identify with the mind are viewed by Lambe as cognitive by-products of the more fundamental activities of brain.

Mathematical Theory and Neural-Net Architecture

Although cognitive scientists have known for two decades that research in neuroscience was providing insights into how to build computers with alternate architectures, the neural-network revolution can properly be said to have begun with the publication in 1982 of a paper entitled "Neural Networks and Physical Systems with Emergent Collective Computational Ability." The author of this paper was John Hopfield, a physicist at the California Institute of Technology, who during the 1960s had studied the properties of silicon and other materials used in constructing computer chips. Sensing that the synergistic interplay between computer-based research in neuroscience and computer science would present new research possibilities, Hopfield began meeting in the 1970s with a select group of cognitive scientists who gathered twice a year at MIT. Drawing on his extensive background in mathematical physics, Hopfield soon began a study of the mathematical properties of networks of interacting neurons.

Hopfield's seminal insight was that networks of neurons in the brain could be analyzed with the same tools physicists use to analyze dynamic physical systems. In dynamic physical systems, like those studied in the physics of chaos, interaction between large numbers of individual elements produces "emergent properties." Hopfield typically illustrates this phenomenon by pointing out that if we put one thousand molecules into a box that previously contained ten molecules, the result is simply more collisions. Yet if we put a billion billion molecules into the same box, we witness the emergent collective property of sound waves. The manner in which the evolving brains of our prehistoric ancestors provided the physical substrate for the information-processing activities we associate with consciousness can also be understood, in part, in these terms.

Our evolutionary history resulted in the survival of organisms with brains containing increasingly larger numbers of neurons. As those numbers became critically large, interaction between groups of neurons resulted in emergent properties that would become the collective basis for consciousness. Since the behaviors made possible by the emergent properties were conducive to survival, consciousness became an evolutionarily advantageous information-processing activity. As Hopfield puts it, "Biology doesn't particularly care where the emergent properties come from. It just uses whatever evolution gives it that happens to work. If emergent properties occur in a particular network of neurons, and evolution can use them for computation, that's all the better."[1]

The mathematical model that Hopfield developed based on the study of actual neural circuits does not explain global brain function. Yet his model is vital to the future of computer science and computer-based research in neuroscience for this reason: it cogently explains computational properties of neural nets in the language of mathematics and physics, or in terms that engineers and computer scientists can readily understand. The result in the short term will be a generation of computer systems with a new range of capabilities and associated applications. What will prove most significant about this development in the longer term is that neural networks make it possible to model how groups of neurons produce the emergent properties associated with human thought and behavior. As biophysicist and cognitive scientist Terry Seynowski puts it, "Neural nets are not just a way of getting answers to old problems. They will also produce new questions. The models represent a new language in which different kinds of researchers can talk about mind and brain."[2]

Principles of Neural-Net Architecture

In Hopfield's model, the manner in which interacting neurons produce an emergent property can be viewed as a physical process in which transfer of energy is decreasing. Like molecules in a heated bar of metal that hardens as it cools, the switches in the neural net turn on and off at random as the neural net goes through a similar stabilizing process. The element of randomness in the initial stages of this processing eventually results in a stable arrangement of the net's on-off switches as the system makes its best-case approximations. The interconnected units in the neural net, like the interconnected neurons in the human brain, act on all the data at once in massively parallel computation. Also like the human brain, the neural nets have no central processing unit.

One way to visualize this process is to imagine that an individual model neuron in a neural net is like a pressure valve set at a certain level in a system of water pipes. If there is enough water pressure from water in other pipes, the pressure valve opens the pipe and the water is sent toward other similar valves. The individual model neuron in the neural net reacts in a similar way. Now correlate pressure with positive and negative numbers, and suppose that a neuron in a network is designed to send its signal when it receives a positive input of 4 or more. If the model neuron receives a signal of 1 from four other such neurons, it sends out its own signal. As this neuron receives input from large numbers of other neurons, say two thousand, it receives lots of different values, like +5 or −3 or no value at all. As the model neuron adds up all these inputs and the incoming messages go over the threshold, it turns off and sends that message to other model neurons to which it is connected. This message might, in turn, affect the state of other neurons to which it is connected, and thus the settling of the interchange of messages continues until the switching stops and the network is stable. The movement is from a high-energy state at the point of receiving the input to a low-energy state where the interacting neurons have settled into a solution. The result is an assortment of related information that is not arrived at in the linear, step-by-step manner of the Von Neumann computer, and the conclusions drawn are emergent properties of the interaction of all the individual neurons.[3]

The analogy between Hopfield's neural net and the human brain can be further extended, in that the key elementary circuit can be viewed as an input "dentrite" and an output "axon." The role of the synapse is represented by a resistor that connects the "axon" of one model neuron to the "dentrite" of another. Thousands of these model neurons connected with one another via resistors form a network, and the connections between the model neurons, like those of actual neurons, are a function of connection strength. What makes this analogy less than exact is that the model neurons connect symmetrically and actual neurons do not. Also, actual neurons fire a series of spiked impulses, are both inhibitory and excitatory, and the parallelism is truly massive. The model neurons, in contrast, respond in an on and off manner, are often excitatory, and the network is only modestly parallel. Yet even at this nascent stage in the neural-network revolution, we confront a technology that could perform a wide new range of tasks heretofore performed only by human beings.

In making this claim, I should emphasize that the neural-net revolution is only in its infancy, and its more mindlike capabilities have yet to be fully demonstrated. In fact, neural-net architecture at the moment is a "weaker" architecture than that of a Von Neumann computer in terms of programming possibilities, and most research on neural nets is being carried out in simulations of neural networks on Von Neumann machines. It is also true that some mindlike tasks, such as grammatical parsing and automated inference, are much more advanced on conventional AI systems than on neural nets.

Yet we would be quite foolish to take a wait-and-see attitude about the range of new applications for neural-net computers in the technological future. What we confront here is a computer architecture that more closely resembles the structure of the human brain, and thus the prospect that this architecture will be better able to simulate the activities of this brain. Whether the prospects for neural-net computers as their developers now conceive them will come to fruition as quickly as they imagine is, of course, unknown. Yet much evidence suggests that the neural-net revolution is a signal event in the movement toward the creation of more mindlike computers—even if the time required to achieve this goal is greater than its promoters imagine.

Mindlike Capabilities of Neural Nets

A prime limitation of the present generation of computers is the manner in which they retrieve and store information in their memories. Each memory has what is called an address, and the computer must move to the address to retrieve the memory. The address is just a number and has no connection to the actual content of the memory stored there. This means that a separate set of instructions must be written for every aspect of the computer's memory-retrieving capabilities. In a neural network, in contrast, storage and retrieval of memory are aspects of the same system, and there is no need for separate instructions for retrieving data. The streams of 1s and 0s are not stored in a set of switches in a separate memory bank. Instead, the resistors in the wires between the model neurons are adjusted so that the network has a variety of resting states that produce the 1s and 0s corresponding to a different string of information or a different memory. What most excites the researchers and developers of neural nets is that this arrangement presents new opportunities for building computers that can more easily form categories and make associations.

When, for example, we think of a friend named John, we might remember that John is a dentist, lives in New Jersey, and has red hair. If someone asks, "Did you say that you knew a redheaded dentist in New York City?" we would have no difficulty responding, "No, New Jersey." Similarly, if we try to recall John's phone number and can remember only the beginning digits "620," this partial information will probably be positioned somewhere in the neuronal organization of our brain so that we can recall the full number. It is this content-addressable aspect of human memory that the neural net can simulate. If one stable set of the neural net's switches represents an assortment of information—as in John, dentist, red hair, New Jersey, and John's phone number—the whole memory can be retrieved by the input of any part of the memory. Hopfield has demonstrated that if we introduce only 5 percent of a memory into a neural net, the system will produce the entire memory. Even when we introduce slightly incorrect information, a neural net can make a best-case approximation with one of its memories.

The ability of the neural net to make best-case approximations, even if the answer is not entirely correct, is also analogous to the functioning of the human mind. Computing all the variables when making decisions is time-consuming and would not have been an efficient survival tool. As Hopfield puts it, "Biology by and large is not interested in finding the best things, just things that are pretty good that can be found quickly."[4] For example, speech experts have estimated that we comprehend only about 70 percent of spoken words, and that our minds manage to fill in the rest based on the content of what is being said. Experiments have also shown that the human mind fills in the blanks based on contextual analysis in visual perception, and that the mind can generate an image based on scant visual data.

To illustrate the new range of applications that neural-net computers make possible, consider a typical optimization task known as the "traveling salesman problem." The salesman in this particular example must visit ten cities in the United States, and the problem is to determine the shortest route to visit all of them at least once. Assume that the possible routes to the ten cities number 181,440. Although it is not too difficult to determine on a traditional computer using heuristic programming which of these 181,440 routes between ten cities is the shortest, the number of possible routes can become staggering as the number of cities to be visited increases. If the total number of cities becomes 100, then we are dealing with something like 10^{100} routes. Although we have developed a number of sophisticated strategies for solving this problem on conventional computers, at some level most still involve time-consuming measurements of each route. If, however, we have a neural net in which resistors can be put in the connections between neurons representing different distances between cities and the order in which they can be visited, we could have a solution in a few millionths of a second. The system would quickly move to its lowest energy state and find one of the shortest routes. In an experiment conducted by Hopfield and David Tank, an associate at AT&T's Bell Labs, the neural network was a thousand times faster in solving a typical "traveling salesman" problem than a conventional computer. The singular advantage that the neural network has over its conventional rival is that it does not consider whether the individual propositions are strictly true or false. Instead, each proposition is a function of the strength of the network's "opinion" as to whether it is true or false, and has weight according to connection strength.[5]

Neural Nets as Research Tools in Cognitive Science

Obviously, there would be no neural-network revolution without the synergistic interplay between computer-based research in neuroscience and computer science. As Carver

Mead, a longtime associate of Hopfield's who was the first to put his neural net on a silicon chip, puts it, "We have a machine to study, the brain, that is the result of millions of years of evolution. What's more, we have the result of these millions of years of evolution to study it with. So there's no point to try to use trial and error to recreate something that we have sitting in front of us." What is being recognized here is that computer-based research in neuroscience has become inextricably connected with research in computer science, and enlarging the capabilities of computer systems is highly dependent upon understanding the information-processing activities of the human brain. As Mead explains the current situation, "No one is even remotely contemplating doing anything remotely like a brain. We're just trying to do little pieces— an artificial retina or cochlea. If we can do just these little pieces, we'd be very happy. It's a start. In another ten or twenty years we can go a long way."[6]

The manner in which the neural net as research tool is serving this effort can be illustrated with a study done by neuroscientists Richard Anderson, at MIT, and David Zisper, at the University of California at San Diego. The intent was to try to determine how the brain is able to precisely locate a visual object based on nerve impulses of signals from the eyes. The researchers first trained a neural network by giving it signals recorded from actual neurons that control the muscles that move the eyes, as well as signals recorded in the retina. Following this training, the neural network eventually learned to judge the position of an object in front of its "eyes." Readings from various neurons in the artificial network revealed that they were quite similar to those in the area of the brain that performs this task. Although what is being modeled here is only one aspect of the complex vision process, the researchers expect that this technique will lead to a much improved understanding of the entire process.[7]

Similarly, neuroscientist David Lynch and his computer-science colleague Richard Granger at the University of California at Irvine have attempted to model the brain's smell circuitry with a neural network. In one experiment, they presented their five hundred model neuron network with two groups of simulated odors that contained variations on a more general pattern represented by "cheese" and "flower." Each simulated odor was represented by a pattern of neural activity: cheese simulated one group of neurons, and flower another group. Initially, the network responded with a unique pattern of activity for each odor. When the network was presented with increasing numbers of examples of similar odors, however, the model neurons repeatedly activated by similar odors became stronger and dampened the activity of less active neurons. The highly active neurons learned and represented the general category within which a group of odors belonged. Old patterns were replaced with new patterns as a result of experience. Since experiments on rats' brains have shown that specific neurons are active in the presence of some smells and not others, Lynch and Granger hope to develop an understanding of the regularities involved in learning and encoding categories of odors.[8]

The list of cognitive scientists who have undertaken related projects is impressively long. For example, Alan Gelperin, from Princeton and AT&T Laboratories, has been working with Hopfield to develop a neural network that might simulate aspects of learning behavior in the nervous system. Terry Seynowski has committed himself to developing a new discipline, dubbed "computational neuroscience," to provide mathematical tools for investigating how neurons collectively process information. Ralph Linsker at IBM's Watson Research Lab in Yorktown, New York, has developed a neural-net simulation to study how the brain of a growing fetus might arrange its wiring to perform visual tasks. And M.D. and cognitive scientist Gerald Edelman, at Rockefeller University, uses a neural net to test assumptions in a theory that he terms "Neural Darwinism." Edelman's fundamental assumption is that in the effort to pass on their genes to subsequent generations, groups of neurons compete with one another for neural pathways in a manner analogous to competition between organisms.[9]

A Model for the Emergent Mind

The best known of the more global computer-science models for brain function has been developed by Marvin Minsky and Seymour Papert at MIT. The fundamental assumption in this model is that the intelligence of future generations of computer systems will not be a single, unified agent, but rather a community of mental agents. As Minsky observes, intelligence for human beings is not in the agents themselves, but rather in their organization, or the manner in which they interact, make alliances, or work together. Just as the word *life* has lost much of its mystery for modern biologists, so will the word *mind*, claims Minsky, lose much of its mystery as cognitive scientists map the neuronal activity in the brain that creates emergent properties like intelligence, insight, creativity, understanding, and so on. The task for cognitive science is, then, to create a computer that operates as a "society of mind," and that can better emulate the interacting neuronal patterns in the wet machine that we associate with consciousness.[10]

In Minsky's view, the evolution of the adult brain, which can use sophisticated logic and operate at high levels of abstraction, begins with a society of individual actors in the brain of a child. These actors first operate under genetic programs linked together through common communication channels and carry out actions with a common database. In the first few months of life many actors or agents work in redundancy on the same task, and pathways corresponding with groups of agents differentiate and specialize as the child matures. Specialized networks of neuronal patterns correspond with the actors, and neighboring networks share communication channels and much of their data as they become more specialized. Networks more removed from one another communicate only in limited ways via other channels and have only limited access to other data. Genetic programming and learning govern the hierarchical process of specialization and allow the brain to develop its overall neuronal structure. The structure that eventually emerges, suggests Minksy, is composed of the simplest actors on the most primitive level of organization, and of actors that employ abstractions, concepts, symbols, and language at the higher levels.[11] The critical feature of Minsky's model is that the principles of organization are not imposed from the top-down or from the outside: they emerge as a collective property of the interaction of individual neurons. And this is precisely what neural networks allow.

Although an AI system worthy of the name "mind-machine" will not emerge soon, there are a number of indications that this technological possibility could become a reality in the foreseeable future. The complex information-processing activities we associate with consciousness could eventually emerge as a collective emergent property of many computing elements in a richly interconnected system. The coloring of thought with the machine equivalent of emotion could also be accomplished, as cognitive science learns to represent this feedback process from the human limbic system with mathematical models appropriate for incorporation into computer systems with alternate architectures. Even the machine equivalent of human subjective reality could emerge as a collective property of a computer system. Here one can envision the machine equivalent of the left brain inference-making system confronting inputs from other systems and attempting to represent them in terms of its own emergent logic and prior experience.

Neural Nets and the Language of Thought

Movement toward this momentous event obviously requires a much improved understanding of how the left brain verbal-processing system and other related systems employ language to represent thought. The approach to understanding language as a basis for cognition that most preoccupied the first generation of AI theorists was developed by Noam Chomsky. In his famous *Logical Structure of Linguistic Theory*, Chomsky challenged the efficacy of the two dominant models for linguistic regularities. The first model, finite-state grammars, assumed that sentences were formed in a linear fashion—one word leads to the selection of a second and third and so on. The second model, phrase-structure grammars, assumed that words were regularly grouped with other words into phrases, and that these phrases could be broken down into subphrases. The object of linguistics, therefore, was to determine in a given language the number and types of phrases that would constitute the complete set of phrases that serve as building blocks of sentences.

Chomsky demonstrated that finite-state grammars simply cannot account for the linguistic content of many sentences, and that phrase-structured grammars suffered similar limitations. His alternative model, transformational grammar, assumes that the *syntax* of language—the logical connections between types of words—could be studied independently of *semantics*—what the words and sentences actually mean. Chomsky's model suggested that the scientific study of language could be conducted in the "abstract," divorced from the speaker of the language. Language, claimed Chomsky, is a system of symbols and the rules that govern how these symbols are used. When traditional linguists after Chomsky have confronted the fact that they have great difficulty explaining language as it is used by actual human speakers, they have typically appealed to the distinction between performance, or language as it is described by linguists, and competence, those deviations from the theoretical system due to the limitations of individual human beings.

In the view of many cognitive scientists, this performance-competence distinction does not hold, because language has no existence in the abstract. Language exists only as it is used by actual speakers, and both the structure and meaning conveyed by language are emergent activities of the information processing of the human brain. George Lakoff at the Univeristy of California at Berkeley is in the vanguard of a new generation of linguists who appeal to work done in cognitive science. One of the principal insights Lakoff derived from cognitive science was that the traditional Western notion of categories was false. This notion, which Lakoff terms the "objectivist" view, assumes that reality is constituted from external objects that have certain properties and external relationships. The objectivist view is represented in traditional linguistics, suggests Lakoff, in the assumptions that a sentence is a series of strings of "uninterpreted" symbols, and that fixed internal relationships give these symbols meaning. Thus, for the traditional linguist the real world looks like a conventional computer database. Lakoff's alternative view is that the real world, or the only such world that can be known by human beings, is an emergent property of the human brain, and thus the symbols we use to represent categories are arbitrarily assigned and the boundaries remain fluid. In his view, the ultimate meaning of categories is a function of the reality-processing system that is a particular human brain, and their boundaries, as well as their interconnections, are fuzzy.

If we assume that categories are emergent properties of brain function, then there must be, reasons Lakoff, a process through which basic categories evolve in particular cultures as a result of the interaction between the world-constructing minds of individuals and their physical and cultural environment. It is Lakoff's conviction that neural networks will eventually be capable of modeling the hidden dynamics of this complex process. Since memories in a neural net represent a pattern of activity among the neurons, future generations of this technology could conceivably model the formation and evolution of categories within a linguistic framework in response to input that corresponds with learning. This means, claims Lakoff, that neural nets could eventually model the language produced by our minds in terms of the structure of our brain. It already seems clear that the patterns of neuronal activity associated with various brain systems interacting with those from other systems are responsible for the higher-level patterns governing perception and motor control. If overlapping and dynamic neuronal patterns also form general patterns representing basic concepts, then patterns of activity that fit one concept should overlay patterns representing other concepts.

Consider, for example, how the following meanings of the word *took* may have been learned: "I took the car" or "I took John home" or "I took a rest" or "I took the blame." Although grafting a new meaning on an old word would appear to be an obvious explanation for how we come to understand these related but slightly different meanings, the classical approach to language fails to explain how this process works. If a neural net is trained on these examples, however, it will add the new connections, or inferences about meaning, over the connections or patterns of meaning that already exist. Reasoning in these terms is not the business of deducing one thing from another; it is a consequence of the evolving dynamic interaction of multiple patterns of interconnection. The rules that might appear to govern the process, like the "laws" of logic, are understood here as emergent aspects of the dynamic organization. In other words, they do not have a prior or separate existence outside of the neuronal activity of individual human brains.[12]

The neural-net model also suggests how the human mind might contextualize verbal information, and how it might develop scenarios for meaning based on scant verbal clues. If someone says, for example, "Mary left work early in order to pick up her Mercedes," we would suppose that Mary is an adult and probably infer that she has a rather good job with some professional autonomy. If, on the other hand, we substitute "used car" or "relief check" for "Mercedes," we would create a very different scenario. Since most of the words we hear or read convey scant contextual information, the listener or reader does most of the fill-in-the-blank construction work. What may happen is that the pattern of meaning that we identify with the spoken or written words is overlaid by patterns of meaning encoded previously, and that the best-case or most meaningful scenario results as the neuronal organization settles to its lowest energy state.

The Connections and Learning Strategies Problems

The neural-net researchers who hope to emulate such activities of the human brain are obviously dealing with a situation in which hundreds or thousands of connections exist in multiple layers, and where manipulating connection strengths to arrive at the best-case pattern match is a formidable challenge. One problem is how to wire hundreds or thousands of connections in a large multilayered net so that the system will arrive at a best-case pattern match at all layers. If the connection strength is set at a level that does not reach all layers, the system could achieve the lowest energy state without moving toward the lowest levels. It was this problem that Terry Seynowski and Geoff Hinton, a neural-net expert now at the University of Toronto, sought to resolve with a system named after the nineteenth-century Austrian physicist Ludwig Boltzman. The basic strategy was to program the mathematical equivalent of "shaking" into a neural net, so that the connection strength that represents a solution on a level that does not link to all hidden inputs moves to a deeper level where this linkage can occur. It is not unlike shaking a marble in a box until it settles at the lowest possible point in the terrain.[13]

When the Boltzman computer is being trained, the strengths of the connections between the hidden units and all the model neurons is set at random. As a result of training, the hidden units come to represent the overall features of the world being modeled. If a particular hidden unit does not continue to be invoked in the repeated problem-solving activity, it simply withers away. The manner in which the Boltzman machine sets up the hidden units to solve a particular problem is variable, and the exact arrangement differs slightly at the end of each trial. The problems that the Boltzman machine seeks to solve, like trying to determine whether a ten-by-ten array of black-and-white squares is symmetrical around a horizontal, vertical, or diagonal axis, may seem more computer-like than mindlike. Yet the problems addressed by this and other neural nets are leading to answers that will enhance our ability to build a more mindlike computer. The essential problem with the Boltzman machine is that learning involves hundreds of trials punctuated by time-consuming relaxations, making the system unbearably slow. Thus the primary outcome of this experiment was the realization that other learning schemes needed to be developed.

The learning schemes for multilayered neural nets fall into three types. The unsupervised learning approach allows the system to organize its hidden units without help from the outside—a set of model neurons compete among themselves for the proper or best-case response to a particular input. In the reinforcement approach, the connections among the model neurons in the hidden layer are randomly laid out and then reshuffled as the network receives feedback on how close it is to solving the problem. The closer the network comes to the best-case solution, the stronger the connections corresponding to this solution. Andy Barto, at the University of Massachusetts, and Richard Sutton, at GTE Labs in Waltham, Massachusetts, have used the reinforcement approach to simulate how a bug finds its way to a tree using a simulation of scent from the tree as a reinforcement guide. These researchers have used this same methodology to train a neural net to control the back-and-forth motions of a rolling cart so that it could balance a pole upright.[14]

Since the randomness featured in unsupervised learning and reinforcement learning is slow and inefficient, a third scheme, called back propagation, has been developed. In this scheme information about errors is filtered back through a multilayered neural net so that the net will adjust the connections between the layers of neurons to improve performance. Although feedback in the neuronal connections of the human brain in the process of learning is obviously an autonomous activity, feedback in back propagation requires that a programmer determine what is and is not a correct input. If neural nets are to better model the actual processes of learning in the human brain, we must develop methodologies that allow the net itself to arrive at best-case solutions on its own.

One promising new approach comes from psychologist John Skoyles of the University College of London. Skoyles assumes that the human brain trains itself in a "bootstrap" fashion—using one network among its different networks to train another. A child, for example, first learns a few simple words on a trial-and-error basis while attempting to read aloud. Information in one network in the child's brain about how these words are pronounced might then be used to train another network to pronounce smaller groups of letters found in the words. Knowledge about how the groups of letters are pronounced might then be used to train yet another network to read by recognizing whole words as opposed to sounding out the letters, and so on. The bootstrap approach assumes that the brain in the learning process climbs a cognitive ladder, training a series of networks of increasing sophistication and "boosting" itself to higher levels of information processing.[15]

Commercial and Military Applications for Neural Nets

In addition to providing a theoretical framework and research tool that allow fundamental questions about the information-processing system of the brain to be raised and answered, the neural-network revolution has also spawned the development of new computer systems with a new range of concrete applications. The competition to develop the best neural network on a silicon chip now involves top scientists and engineers at AT&T, TRW, Texas Instruments, IBM, General Electric, and NASA's Jet Propulsion Laboratory. Major computer firms in Europe and Japan have dedicated similar talents and resources to this effort, and more than two hundred start-up companies have entered the competition over the last two years. For example, a $15,000 circuitboard that can simulate a neural network when interfaced with a conventional computer is now being marketed by SAIC Technological Research in San Diego. Similarly, TRW now markets a commercial version of a neural-net simulator that it had developed earlier for DARPA.

Aware of the potential military applications of neural-net technology, the U.S. Department of Defense announced in 1988 that it intended to spend $400 million to support a wide range of neural-net projects over a period of eight years. A neural net under development at Allied-Signal has, for example, already been trained to recognize underwater targets based on the objects' reflections of sonar signals. Similarly, an optical neural net developed at the University of Pennsylvania uses radar signals from various vehicles to target particular vehicles based on as little as 10 percent of the radar pattern.[16] Neural-net technology is also being employed in DARPA's $1 billion Strategic Computing Program. Announced in 1985, the Strategic Computing Program originally intended to make the following systems operational within ten years: an autonomous land vehicle, a pilot's associate, and a naval carrier group battle-management system.

The autonomous land vehicle is a completely autonomous robot that would be capable of resupply, ammunition handling, and weapons delivery. Early versions of the robot are expected to have wheels and move on roadways, while later versions are expected to have mechanical legs like a huge insect. The system should also be capable of recognizing and responding to information about objects in three-dimensional space. The pilot's associate is a computer capable of taking over the task of flying a bomber or a jet fighter, leaving the human pilot free to perform tasks like those on a bombing run. This computer system would also take over control of the aircraft when fired upon by an interceptor missile and would conduct evasive maneuvers at accelerations that cause a human being to black out. The associate would also be able to understand a two-hundred-word vocabulary from any speaker, so that the human pilot could verbally instruct the computer, thus leaving the pilot's hands free to perform other tasks.

The naval group battle-management project aims to develop a system that can display a detailed picture of a battle, including the enemy order of battle (surface, air, and subsurface), its own force disposition, the electronic-warfare environment, strike plan, and weather forecasts. The system would also be able to generate hypotheses about the enemy's possible intentions, rank them in terms of likelihood, and indicate the best possible outcome for each course of response. After a course of action occurs, the system would prepare and generate the operating plan throughout the fleet and monitor the outcome. The project goals for voice recognition on this system call for recognition and interpretation of sentences spoken in a ten-thousand-word vocabulary in natural grammar by any speaker.[17] Although the goals of all these projects are incredibly ambitious and will not be realized within the projects' original time frames, it is nevertheless likely, given the amount of human and capital resource involved, that substantial progress will be made.

Efforts to solve the problem of speech recognition are also being vigorously pursued for commercial applications. Hect-Nielsen Neurocomputer, Votan, and Synaptics are working on voice recognition systems, and IBM and AT&T are rumored to have been doing so for some time.

Votan is already test marketing a neural-net system that can recognize numbers spoken over the phone for applications involving credit card companies and banks. Similarly, Nestor, Inc., has developed a neural-net type design that can run on an IBM PC and that reads handwritten characters written on a pen-sensitive pad; the company has also developed a network-based program to recognize any of 2,500 handwritten Japanese characters.

Neural Nets as Mindlike Evaluators and Decision Makers

The ability of neural nets to make associations and generalizations based on a complex set of data and to arrive at best-case approximations in solving fuzzy problems is also quickly leading to commercial applications. Neural nets, like the one in use at a financial service company in Irvine, California, have already proved themselves capable of performing some routine tasks of evalution better than conventional computers. After the company used a neural net to assess the credit worthiness of applicants for loans, it compared the results to those of a computer program that had previously assessed credit worthiness. The conclusion was that profits would have been 27 percent higher if the neural network had been used instead. What this evidence suggests is that neural networks could become cost effective in performing routine tasks of evaluation, and that many human beings who now perform these tasks will be displaced.

It is, however, the potential applications of neural nets in areas like crisis management, or in social science applications for the government or the military, that should be our greatest concern. If it is possible to use neural nets to model the role played by association and analogy within the context of evaluation and decision-making paradigms, we should reasonably expect that AI systems could play a much larger role than they do at present in the management of human affairs. We would then have a technology that could model and predict attitudes and behaviors impacting such diverse phenomena as the salability of new products and services, economic trends, the outcomes of elections, the effects of new public policy, and whether nuclear war might result from a particular military action.

Although no AI system at present can begin to realistically model the manner in which complex variables impact decision making and behaviors in any of these areas, we can imagine how such systems might evolve. One of the most difficult problems in anthropology is to achieve an understanding of how fundamental features of a culture originated. The ability of the neural net to proceed through trial and error toward generalization could allow anthropologists to introduce environmental or cultural variables into a simulated environment and to observe the underlying structures that emerge in the net as it arrives at a best-case solution. Neural nets have already provided insights into such underlying structures in language, as they learn to change verbs from past to present tense.

Similarly, the emergence of underlying structures in a single domain of human reality could be modeled and better understood through a group of neural nets employing different computational systems that have learned to operate and continually interact within a simulation of this aspect of reality. The fundamental assumption in such research programs would be that a society consists of a collection of individual information-processing systems, or minds, that employ specialized computational systems, or evaluation and decision-making paradigms. If we could build such a system, then what we term ideas, opinions, and values could compete with and reinforce each other in a sea of richly complex variables associated with a large and enlarging set of previously learned computational patterns. Aron Cicourel, a sociologist at the University of California at San Diego, is now using an early version of such a model to study the manner in which physicians rely on various computational systems in making diagnoses.[18]

Whether this progress will be painfully slow or very fast will depend in large part on the progress made in computer-based research in neuroscience. If this research leads to the development of a mathematical model that serves to explain global or holistic aspects of brain function, then a conscious computer by the Turing criteria could lie well within the range of the technological feasibility. When we also factor into this equation some anticipated developments on the hardware side of the computer industry, which will be discussed in the next chapter, this prospect seems even more likely.

CHAPTER 5
The Birth of the Mindlike Computer

A shape with lion body and the head of a man,
A gaze blank and pitiless as the sun,
Is moving its slow thighs, while all about it
Reel shadows of the indignant desert birds.
The darkness drops again; but now I know
That twenty centuries of stony sleep
Were vexed to nightmare by a rocking cradle,
And what rough beast, its hour come round at
*   last*
Slouches towards Bethlehem to be born?
                                —W. B. Yeats
                                    "The Second Coming"

When in 1921 the Irish poet Yeats forecast a radical transformation in the emotional and intellectual makeup of human beings that was to be complete around the year 2000, he obviously was not thinking about computer technologies. The metaphor Yeats chose to describe this transformation, the rough beast with the body of a lion and the head of a man, represents a human nature in which the balance has shifted dramatically away from the qualities of intuition, sympathy, and acceptance and toward coldly analytical thought and calculated aggression. The rough beast whose potential existence will concern us in this chapter is not a metaphor. Although a computer capable of passing the Turing test will certainly not come into existence by the year 2000, it is conceivable that a computer that learns from experience, and that relies extensively upon analogy and associative reasoning, could be operational in that year. And it is also possible that a massively parallel system based on neural-net or other similar architectures will display the machine equivalent of human emotion and human subjective reality not long thereafter.

When a computer passes the Turing test, most of the important questions regarding what is implied by this event already will have been decided. We may already have projected onto AI computer systems ideas, assumptions, attitudes, and values that may not prove in the best interests of human survival or of maintaining the quality of human life. It is also conceivable that the qualities Yeats feared would become dominant in human nature could be dominant in the emergent consciousness of AI computer systems.

Based on the advances that have been made over the past few decades in theoretical physics and biophysics, the next frontier of complexity in science, complex biological processes, could be crossed within a fifty-year time frame. If that occurs, and if we have a mathematical model for global brain function, such a model would almost certainly be used in the construction of a more mind-like computer. The distance between theory and practice will be measured in terms of exponential increases in computational ability and processing speed, the ability to construct more neuronlike connections, and vastly more sophisticated neural-network or yet-to-be-invented architectures.

Given the importance of AI systems in the competition between nation-states for economic and political hegemony, resources for AI system development are not likely to be a problem. The capabilities of the next, or fifth, generation of computer technologies have been described by Edward Feigenbaum and Pamela McCorduck:

> This new generation of computers will be more powerful than any other the world has seen—indeed, by orders of magnitude. But their real power will not lie in their processing speed, but in their capacity to reason. . . . These new computers, which users will be able to speak to in everyday conversational language, or show pictures to, or transmit to by keyboard or by handwriting, [will] penetrate every level of society. They will assume no special expertise or knowledge of arcane programming languages. They will not even require the user to be very specific about his needs, because they will have reasoning power, and will be able to tease out from the user, by questioning and suggestions, just exactly what it is the user wants to know. Finally, these new machines will be inexpensive enough and reliable enough to be used everywhere, in offices, factories, restaurants, shops, farms, fisheries, and, of course, homes.[1]

Since national security is also perceived as critically dependent on the development of new AI technologies, we can anticipate dramatic increases in the levels of capital investment in this area. All of which means that we will embark soon, if we have not already done so, on a project similar to the Manhattan Project or the Apollo space program in the following respects: massive amounts of capital resources and the best minds in all related fields will be devoted to solving complex technological problems in an effort to win a "war" with enormous geopolitical consequences. The winner in this round will be the nation that produces the most cost-effective and efficient fifth-generation artificial intelligence computers.

The Connections and Number of Units Problems

The enormous increases in the computational power of the computer have resulted primarily from the microminiaturization of its fundamental unit, the switch. If we are to meet the computational needs of communications, complex image-processing, and scientific research in the 1990s, new generations of superfast, multimillion transistor chips will be required. Yet if these chips are manufactured, there are two fundamental natural barriers that must be overcome: the quantum tunneling effect and Ohm's law. Quantum tunneling represents a barrier because the insulator thickness on the most sophisticated chips has now reached a scale, around 25 angstroms, where this peculiar dynamic of subatomic processes comes into play. On these scales electrons manifest in terms of two complementary aspects, wave and particle, in accordance with the indeterminacy principle. What this means is that if the distance that electrons travel in the on-off structure of the switch is equivalent to or less than the wave function of the electron, then the particle aspect of the electron can randomly appear outside the barrier within which it had previously been contained. It is as if the electron in its wave aspect can tunnel through the barrier represented by distances between switches, and convey its yes-no message without our being able to control the process. Ohm's law is viewed as a potential barrier in the further microminiaturization of chips because it decrees that resistance increases in proportion to the reduction in size of the cross section of a conductor. What this means is that further microminiaturization of switches could create higher resistance, and thus slow down the speed of the signals propagating through the chips.

The most promising approach to overcoming these barriers is a dynamic in nature called superconductivity. We have known since 1911 that superconductivity is a property of certain metals when chilled to nearly absolute zero ($-459°$ F). The recent excitement about superconductivity began when IBM scientists discovered in April of 1986 that it can be achieved at higher temperatures by using a class of compounds called ceramic oxides. In February

1987, Paul Chu and his colleagues at the University of Houston and the University of Alabama created a compound capable of superconductivity at the then record high temperature of −283° F. This was significant because the temperature was above the boiling point for liquid nitrogen, a cheap and easily obtainable coolant. What excites computer scientists about these developments is that superconductivity increases the speed of electrons moving through the chips and decreases the resistance of metallic conductors by reducing the thermal vibrations of the electron. It is these properties of superconductivity that suggest that it may be a way of circumventing both the quantum tunneling effect and Ohm's law in the further microminiaturization of chips. Superconductivity could also serve as the basis for a completely new circuit design, in which electricity circulates in a closed loop indefinitely.

Prior to these developments, IBM had been working on superconductor-based switching devices in its Josephson junction project. A Josephson junction operates fifty times faster than state-of-the-art silicon transistors and ten times faster than the best semiconductor devices made of gallium arsenide. It also generates very little heat and uses currents that are ten times lower than those found in conventional transistors. This means that Josephson circuits can be placed very close together in the effort to achieve extra speed. The IBM project began in the mid-1960s, was cosponsored by the Department of Defense, involved 115 researchers at its peak, and had an annual budget of $20 million. Superconductivity at higher temperatures could make the Josephson design cost-effective, and IBM is now rumored to have some one hundred scientists working on various aspects of superconductivity. AT&T's Bell Labs is also pursuing research projects comparable to those of IBM, and several Japanese computer manufacturers—NEC, NTT, Toshiba, and Fujitsu—have active programs. Also, Japan's Ministry of International Trade and Industry (MITI) has put together a consortium to study applications of the new high-temperature superconductors.

What we can reasonably anticipate within five to ten years is a new generation of integrated circuit in which both active elements and connections are fabricated entirely out of superconducting materials.[2]

Another technology in the development stage that should allow us to create more sophisticated chips is x-ray lithography. X-rays are an extremely energetic form of light, with wave lengths shorter than those of ultraviolet light, and electrons that have previously been used in the form of beams to mask the wafers in one of the two hundred steps involved in chip manufacture. The intense beam of x-rays required in lithography can be produced in an electron storage ring, or synchrotron, which was originally developed as a research tool in particle physics. The only x-ray lithography project in the United States, estimated to cost over $1 billion by the time it reaches full production, has been undertaken by IBM. Japan, in contrast, has twenty such projects underway, relying on the use of a dozen synchrotrons. Like most of Japan's major research projects, the x-ray lithography program is a cooperative effort involving major manufacturers and funding from various governmental agencies. A similar project involving major computer manufacturers and funding support from government agencies is also going forward in Europe under the auspices of the Joint European Silicon Initiative (JESI).

The connections problem for collective-decision circuits like those used in neural nets could be solved in a more dramatic fashion with optical computers. Light in the form of laser beams is ideal for implementation on neural-net computers because no wires are needed to move information from one model neuron to large numbers of other such neurons, and the messages between model neurons can cross one another's path without interference. Equally important, laser beams can carry greater amounts of information between model neurons per unit of time. The key feature of the optical computer is a solid-state device called a transphasor that can switch states one thousand times faster than the most advanced transistors. In a conventional computer a transistor accepts only one signal at a time. A transphasor is essentially a nonlinear device—multiple signals can be sent to the device and separated as they emerge. Thus the transphasor makes it possible to process several different laser beams of information simultaneously, or to have information channels that constantly diverge and converge.

In addition to this intrinsic ability to carry out parallel processing on the level of single circuit elements, an optical computer could also work with information in more than two states. Transistors have only two states, conducting and nonconducting. Since a transphasor can switch through a variety of states, like conducting, partly conducting, nonconducting, and so on, it should enhance the ability of neural nets to solve problems by association and analogy as they learn from experience. This means that the optical computer could be a massively parallel, extremely fast machine that is potentially more capable than the current generation of AI computers of dealing with the fuzzy problems of valuation.

Demetri Psaltis of the California Institute of Technology and Nabil Farhat of the University of Pennsylvania have created working prototypes of optical collective circuits.[3] Psaltis has also recently developed a working prototype of an optical neural net that emulates the associative character of human visual memory. After an image is presented to this net in the form of a hologram, the system can produce the entire image based on only partial information. In one experiment, Psaltis gave his optical neural net inputs corresponding to the holographic images of a number of human faces, and then tested its memory with input corresponding to half of one of these faces. Based on this limited input, the net was able to construct the remainder of a particular face.

What is most significant about Psaltis's experiment is that the same principles can be used to construct communication links on optical neural nets. Since a huge amount of data can be stored in a hologram, and since each part of a hologram can be used to connect model neurons together on a neural net, these systems could be very effective in emulating the random problem-solving activities of the human brain. One example of a fairly immediate application for such systems is for matching a particular set of fingerprints with one among millions of other such prints. Since the randomness of fingerprints is such that we have never been able to discover rules that make one set of fingerprints different from another, the only way fingerprints can be matched on conventional computers is by sifting through all the fingerprints stored in the computer's memory. Since an optical neural net in this application would fuse the operations of memory storage and retrieval via the connection strength methodology discussed earlier, it could find a match among millions of other prints very quickly.

We should also note that MITI's $82 million project in optoelectronics, which ended in 1986, resulted in optical sensors and semiconductor lasers that have already been used in products like laser printers, copiers, fax machines, and optical disks. And research groups at NEC, Hitachi, and Fujitsu are now hard at work in the effort to replace the mirrors and lenses in these products with holographic components. In the longer term, neural-net optical computers also could become an effective tool for developing a computer with the machine equivalent of a visual reality and associative visual memory.

The largest obstacle on the hardware side to constructing a computer that can pass the Turing test is likely to be the number of units problems. Consciousness as an emergent property of the human brain was made possible in natural evolution by the appearance of a large number of neurons that evinced collective properties that would not have been present in the interaction of fewer numbers of neurons. And it is safe to assume that the same will be true for the evolution of the conscious computer. This precondition is likely to remain even if a computer capable of passing the Turing test does not require the human brain's 10 billion units and 100 trillion connections. The difference is that the conscious computer, in contrast with the information-processing system of the human brain, could distribute many of its functions, and it would not need to devote enormous amounts of processing power to biologically relevant tasks. On the other hand, such a computer will require many more processing units than are available in current technology. One technology that could conceivably solve this problem is the organic data processor, also known as the biochip. A biochip is a microprocessor built out of complex organic molecules, rather than nonorganic materials like silicon. From the point of view of cognitive science, neuron units and connections are natural biochips.

Computing on the Molecular Level

A biochip, which is now only a theoretical possibility, would be a molecular electronics switching array in which a lengthy string of organic molecules forms between peptide anchor sites on the sides of antibodies. The upper and lower parts could be joined by a switching apparatus that allows the two antibodies to pass signals. The "gate" that allows signals to pass through the device might be an enzyme. The current generation of computer chips requires large ovens to bake silicon chips; e-beams, or high energy beams of electrons, to carve patterns on the silicon; and painstakingly drawn masks to photolithograph patterns on the oxidized disks. If we can achieve a better understanding of the mechanisms via which organic life forms reproduce on the molecular level, we might eventually be able to manipulate these mechanisms to produce biochips.

The bits of information on such a chip could represent a millionfold increase over silicon chips: 50 to 100 billion bits as opposed to 50,000 to 100,000. This means that a library containing ten volumes for every human being on the face of the earth could be stored in a space of roughly one cubic centimeter, with ample storage left for new volumes. Such a chip could also operate on the order of 10 billion times faster than any advanced home computer in use today. There is also no reason, in principle, why a biochip could not "interface" with the neurons of the brain. (The National Science Foundation has funded research on ways in which to interface biochip proteins with neurons since 1982.) Although the creation of biochips may seem impossibly futuristic, a number of current developments suggest that it is a technological possibility.

Langmuir-Blodgett molecular-lithographic chambers are devices in which molecules with conductive, insulative, and other properties are laid out to form a kind of molecular sandwich. Experiments conducted in these chambers attempt to manipulate known molecular properties of the molecular layers so that they can function as the equivalent of electrical gates and memory storage and transfer devices. Companies in the United States and Japan are now experimenting with the chambers in the hope of manufacturing three-dimensional computing devices that could duplicate the computational power of one thousand Cray supercomputers within the space of a cubic centimeter. When we consider that Cray supercomputers weigh several tons and cost roughly $20 million each, we can begin to appreciate what breakthroughs in this research program could represent. In the next phase of this research, it is likely that an effort will be made to modify and assemble the necessary molecules with bacteria. Bacteria are now working as chemical engineers in the gene-splicing industry, where companies like Genentech use vats of genetically engineered bacteria to create insulin, human growth hormone, interferon, and other pharmaceutical products. There are many ways in nature in which atoms are altered in bonding, charge, or other aspects, and thereby change from one state to another, not unlike the basic on-off or 1-0 states of a computer.

For example, the protein rhodopsin, found in the retinal rods that line the back of the eye, undergoes a change of state when struck by light and returns to its previous state after it sends a message to the optical nerve. Assigning the unexposed rhodopsin the value of 0, and the light-exposed rhodopsin a value of 1, a laser could theoretically be used to encode binary information on a surface coated with these proteins. Similarly, a laser could be used to read this information with a reversal mechanism, so that the laser would reset the bit to its original state. Robert Birge, the director of the Center for Molecular Electronics at Carnegie-Mellon University, is now researching this methodology.

In order to appreciate the orders of magnitude increase in computing power, speed, and density in computers operating on the molecular level, we might pause to consider what standard measures of length on the molecular level—micron, nanometer, and angstrom—represent in terms of one meter:

one micron = a millionth of a meter;
one nanometer = one billionth of a meter;
one angstrom = one 10-billionth of a meter.

A typical cell is about ten microns across, and a typical rhodopsin measures about fifty angstroms by fifty angstroms.

A five-and-a-quarter-inch floppy disk coated with rhodopsin could in theory hold some 200 million megabytes, and switch from state A to B in one billionth of a second—many orders of magnitude faster than a magnetic medium is capable of switching. Assuming that laser technology progressed to the point at which it was capable of writing on each molecule, one typical floppy could store as much as ten million twenty-megabyte hard disks. If this technology is developed, it will not, of course, be on floppy disks or other magnetic media. It will have its own unique configuration and be packaged at much greater densities. Companies like Genex Corporation, which specializes in gene-splicing technology, are now engaged in the development of molecular electronic devices, and rumor has it that the Japanese are pursuing basic research in this area on a large scale.

Of particular interest for these researchers are the ribosomes, which are capable of reading instructions from RNA within cells and of stringing together amino acids to build thousands of different varieties of proteins. The ribosome is itself composed of seventy different proteins and is capable of reassembling itself when taken apart. If the mechanisms of this self-assembling process can be understood, it may be a key to creating complex molecular structures with computational ability. Assuming that biophysics masters this frontier of complexity, the principles of self-organization and self-synthesis in the realm of biology will be applied in the creation of new inorganic and organic substances. These substances could also have the specific properties needed to function in computers at densities higher than that which we find in the neuronal organization of the human brain.

The Computer as Life Form

One of the most brilliant and imaginative of theoreticians on this new frontier of computer research is Eric Drexler of MIT's Artificial Intelligence Laboratory. Drexler, like virtually all the best cognitive scientists, is knowledgeable in an impressive number of fields, ranging in his case from quantum mechanics, fiber optics, lasers, and superconductivity to the engineering feats of ants and the flow of pigment grains within the surface cells of flounders. Drexler believes that electronic switches might be built out of the tensioned rods of carbon atoms, which have greater strength than a diamond and which are so small that a mechanical computer built from these rods could fit into the volume of a cell.

Similarly, random-access memory might take the form of a molecular computer tape made of modified polyethylene, in which the fluorine atom represents a 1 and the hydrogen atom a 0. This molecular device could theoretically store two times 10^{25} bits per kilogram—the equivalent of all the books in the Library of Congress—in a space less than a tenth of a millimeter on a side. In other words, the contents of the world's largest library could fit into a space roughly the size of a grain of sand. Drexler has also theorized the materials and methods for producing a molecular computer with a robotic arm that could move around the cell to repair DNA, as well as build other structures.

In a paper for the National Academy of Sciences, Drexler presents a chart showing how naturally occurring substances, like collagen, can function as cables, and how microtubules can function as struts and beams to combine a molecular computer and robotic chassis into a cell-repair machine. He also lists the biological equivalents of bearings, drive shafts, motors, pumps, and pipes that could be employed in the creation of molecular robots.[4] The first step would be to manipulate the known mechanisms of the ribosomes, which already function as a numerically controlled machine for building proteins. The idea would be to manage and control these processes in the construction of a robotic vehicle based on principles known to exist in biological systems. The first generation of these tiny futuristic robots might custom-assemble atoms to build new kinds of computers and other robots that cannot be built from the amino acid parts found in the cells. It is at this stage that the carbon rod computers could be built. This procedure, suggests Drexler, could allow us to produce an entire vehicle, with complete on-board computer, propulsion system, and robotic arm, about the size of a bacterium. This robot would occupy one thousandth of the volume of a roughly ten-micron cubicle cell, and its robotic arm would be some hundred nanometers, or a tenth of a micron long.[5]

Obviously, Drexler's development program will require massive amounts of knowledge that we do not have, particulary in the areas of molecular biology and biophysics. If we do acquire that knowledge, during the same time frame

that we are mapping the more global electrical and biochemical processes of the brain in mathematical detail, we
could face some awesome possibilities. Drexler's computer
would fit into a single cubic micron and be roughly the size
of a single synapse in the human brain. The clock speed
on this particular microcomputer could be on the order of
nanoseconds, as opposed to the milliseconds required for
an action potential between neurons in the human brain
to form a synapse. What this means is that the equivalent
of a computer could replace the neuron, which functions
essentially like a switch, and the whole assemblage of
computers could run by a factor of roughly one million
times faster than the human brain.

The Computer Designs Itself

At some point in this progress, possibly at the sixth computer generation, AI systems in research and development
could be more expert than human beings. Thus the increase in knowledge could proceed at a rate in excess of
that which could be accomplished by human experts
alone. One early indication that we are moving in this
direction has been the effort by MITI, beginning some
thirteen years ago, to develop a computer that can write
its own software. Although the latest effort of this kind, a
$200 million project known as Sigma, did not result in a
computer that can program itself, MITI unhesitatingly
committed another $36 million to the project. A computer
learning at a rate five hundred times faster than a human
being could accomplish in one year what might have otherwise required five hundred years to accomplish. Or, put
more in the economic measures used in research and development, one person-year of this computer would be the
equivalent of five hundred "consecutive" person-years for
a human being.

It has been estimated that no human mathematician, no
matter how bright and dedicated that individual might be,
can assimilate more than roughly one-tenth of the existing knowledge in mathematics, and cannot possibly keep

pace with all advances in the field. A computer system that was expert in higher mathematics might not suffer from such limitations, and it could tirelessly apply its mathematical knowledge to the resolution of new problems. Although this dedicated system need not have all the capabilities of the human brain to perform its tasks, its discoveries could rapidly lead toward the creation of a more mindlike system.

Given the enormous talent and resources that are now being devoted to researching and developing artificial intelligence systems, it is conceivable that the computer will be the driving or dominant force in the creation of the next generation of computers in twenty years. This could mean that all current estimates of the generational advance of computers may be totally inadequate for predicting generational advances in the future. The reasonable assumption is that we are likely to witness an exponential increase in the sophistication of AI technologies, and that the time between computer generations will be reduced dramatically. Taizo Nishikawa, MITI's deputy of industrial electronics, has announced that the successor to their fifth generation project will be a project dedicated to building a "neurocomputer" that simulates more aspects of the structure of the human brain.[6]

What we can also reasonably expect in the foreseeable future are new artificial intelligence systems with dedicated functions that will be increasingly relied upon to manage production and information systems. Given the enormous importance of generational advances in AI systems in economic and geopolitical terms, the resources available for research and development of these systems should increase exponentially. Since theoretical and technical advances in neuroscience and biophysics should also be increasingly perceived as vital to the future of computer technology—as they are already perceived as vital to the future of gene-splicing technologies—the capital resources available for research in these areas could similarly increase.

Hans Moravec is also confident that capital resources

will not be a problem in the development of advanced robotic technologies. Within ten years, claims Moravec, we can anticipate the appearance of a general purpose robot that "will come from the factory with a sufficient set of mechanical, sensory, and control capabilities that can be conveniently invoked by software specially written for particular applications"[7] (see Figure 13). Since this robot could be no more expensive than a small car not long after it appears, and since its software-driven applications will be virtually limitless, he anticipates that it will be common in factories and in the performance of many routine tasks now performed by human beings. The following is Moravec's description of how this general-purpose robot might be constructed based on current technologies:

> It moves on five leg-wheels of the Hitachi design and has two arms with Salisbury hands. Topped with a pair of color TV cameras, it has an unobtrusive array of sonar sensors to sense the world in directions not covered by the cameras. It carries an inexpensive laser gyroscope to help with navigation, and it is controlled by a computer system able to do at least a billion calculations per second. Integral with the computer hardware is a software operating system that allows multiple simultaneous processes. Built-in programs permit objects in the world to be described, visually identified in or out of the clutter, and picked up. A navigational system can be used to build, store, retrieve, and compare maps of the surroundings and to bring the robot to specific locations.[8]

Moravec has also forecast that a robot with reasoning abilities considerably in excess of our own will exist within fifty years, even though its perceptual and motor skills will only be "comparable." In making his own rather convincing case that such a robot will exist within this time frame, he reminds us that modern robotics is only some twenty years old, and that it has only been for the last ten years that computers have been routinely

Figure 13

Sealing and bonding robot.

Laser-welding robot.

Material-handling robot.

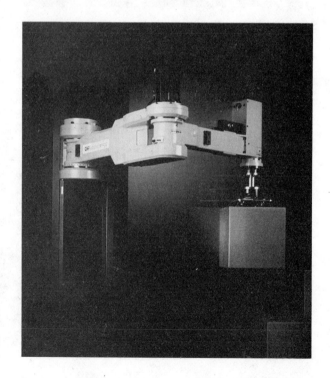

Packaging
robot.

available to control the activities of robots. If Moravec's view of the future of robotics seems unrealistic, consider the PC that Apple Computer anticipates will be available before the end of the century. This system, says Apple's research and development group, will be able to generate full-motion video and animation, to speak and understand speech, to reason through artificial intelligence, and to instantly link its user with any person or information bank in the world. Although we can safely assume that if this system does in fact "understand speech" and "reason," it will do so only in a very rudimentary fashion, this does not obviate the fact that progress in these areas is anticipated to be very rapid.

When a computer passes the Turing test, those who receive the news are not likely to be greatly surprised—we will already have had countless demonstrations that computers can simulate numerous aspects of human consciousness. It is also reasonable to expect that the usual human tendency to anthropomorphize will lead many of us to confer some sense of self on these computers. The important issue will have already been decided: how we have chosen to restructure systems of production, communication, and defense with the use of advanced and advancing AI computer systems. Since AI systems will probably become more expert than we are in particular applications, in almost direct proportion to their more central and vital role in the management of other computer systems, the balance of decision-making power could shift toward the AI systems. These systems could, in short, become more autonomous.

Equally important, there are technologies in the research and development phase that could exponentially increase the range and complexity of the information-processing capabilities of the coming generations of AI systems. These technologies also provide substantive validity for the claims made by the advocates of the AI evolution-of-consciousness hypothesis. Massively parallel optical computers built on neural-net architectures could become the basis for the first generation of AI systems that are demonstrably more capable of complex problem solving in any dedicated area than human intelligence. This development would reinforce the advocates' assumption that the emergent consciousness of AI computer systems is becoming more capable than the human brain.

AI systems that perform complex dedicated tasks more efficiently than human intelligence would undoubtedly be used to solve problems that would allow for further exponential increases in the information-processing capabilities of their descendants. It is likely that AI systems at this stage would become primarily responsible for designing and programming their descendants. It is also safe to assume that the problem solving of conscious AI computers at this stage would involve disclosing and describing in mathematical—or full scientific—detail the complex molecular processes associated with the self-replication and growth of organic life forms, as well as the physical substrates of human consciousness.

What this would mean, in accordance with the hypothesis, is that AI systems will evolve beyond the point at which they will be capable of designing descendants that can emulate any aspect of human consciousness conducive to their own survival. They will continue to evolve until they are capable of producing these descendants through some form of self-replication. The more extreme advocates of the hypothesis argue that when we reach this stage of the evolutionary process, the vastly superior consciousness of self-replicating AI systems will displace the human brain as the physical substrate for consciousness in our corner of the universe.

Yet if developments in the technological future do appear likely to validate the AI evolution-of-consciousness hypothesis, it will not be because they are scripted by the lawful dynamics of the evolution of the cosmos. It will be because human consciousness was enticed into conferring more value in economic and geopolitical terms on its most advanced technological products than it was able or willing to confer on itself. For reasons I will attempt to make clear later, it is human beings who will collectively write the script for this particular drama, and human beings who must accept full responsibility for the results. For the moment, however, let us address what remains the most perplexing question regarding the AI evolution-of-consciousness hypothesis for those of us who have not been thoroughly inducted into the culture of scientists-engineers.

Since the ultimate value of human life and consciousness is typically regarded by the vast majority of us as an ultimate value, why do the advocates elect to believe in the hypothesis, much less arduously seek to prove its validity in scientific terms? The most expedient way to answer this question is to examine the responses of the advocates to systematic attempts by humanists–social scientists to undermine the hypothesis with "what computers cannot do" arguments. One reason why the advocates are not impressed with these arguments is that they are premised in part on an understanding of the present state of AI computer technologies that is either dated or lacking in sophistication. The more fundamental reason why the advocates tend to dismiss these arguments out of hand, however, has to do with some profound differences between how members of these respective intellectual cultures have been trained or taught to evaluate the "truth" value of any proposition. Understanding these differences will also serve to explain why the present state of the dialogue between the two cultures regarding the proper uses of AI technologies cannot even realistically be described as a dialogue. Meaningful dialogues require that the participants play by the same rules of discourse and accept the same standards for what constitutes valid or admissible evidence. There is no meaningful dialogue in this particular debate because the preconditions for such a dialogue simply do not exist.

CHAPTER 6

The Ultimate Man-Machine Interface: Who Shall Make the Journey to the Stars?

*The cosmological argument, which survived
the shift from the Ptolemaic to Newtonian
cosmos, is hopelessly strained between the
unimaginable macrocosm of super-stellar
astronomy and the inscrutable microcosm of
particle physics. And the theological argument
(i.e., many things—e.g., the human eye—are
inextricably designed for purposive ends; ergo,
a directing intelligence exists) was administered
a mortal blow when Darwin demonstrated how
the organic world, for all its seemingly
engineered complexity, might be a self-
winnowing chaos.*
　　　　—John Updike
　　　　"Faith in Search of Understanding"

Hans Moravec invites us to imagine that we are undergoing the following futuristic operation, which he terms
"downloading." A robotic surgeon has opened your skull
and directs his attention "to a small lump of about 100
neurons somewhere near the surface. The three-dimensional structure and chemical makeup of that clump are

determined nondestructively with high resolution 3-D nuclear resonance holography, phased array encephalo-
graphy, and ultrasonic radar. The robotic surgeon then
writes a program that models the behavior of the clump,
and starts it running on a small portion of the computer
next to you." As each area of your brain is analyzed and
simulated, you are able to check the accuracy of the simulation by pressing a button. This procedure shifts your
awareness from the area of your own brain that has been
copied to the representation of the neuronal activity of that
area in computer code. When you have determined that
there is no difference between the two, the robotic surgeon
will perform the same procedure on the next brain area.
"The process," writes Moravec, "is repeated over and over
until the entire brain has been dealt with. Occasionally
several simulations are combined into a single equivalent
but more efficient program. Though you have not lost consciousness, or even your train of thought, your mind—
some would say your soul—has been removed from the
brain and transferred to the machine. . . . In a final step
your old body is disconnected. The computer is installed in
a shiny new one, in the style, color, and material of your
choice."[1] In order to focus more narrowly on the fundamental question raised by the prospect of downloading,
also suppose that the neuronal organization of your brain
associated with all prior experience with language and in
human culture would cease to exist at the point at which
the transfer is complete. Assume that this will occur by
pressing a final button that burns out, or erases, all such
neuronal patterns.

   If we are convinced that human life and consciousness
are nothing more than information-processing activities,
and that what we call "self" is equivalent to emergent
properties of the neuronal activity of our brain, then
downloading, even in my modified version of the procedure, is an attractive prospect. Since consciousness on this
new nonorganic substrate would not be programmed to
return to an inorganic state—to die—it could become vir-

tually immortal. The prospect of immortality could be even more enhanced if we also assume that the dynamic patterns that allegedly constitute our consciousness could be transferred to yet another physical substrate in the event that the one on which they currently reside shows signs of malfunction or deterioration. On the other hand, if we are convinced that our self or conscious being cannot exist on a physical substrate other than that provided by natural or Darwinian evolution, downloading as I have described it is anything but an attractive prospect. Although the human organism left behind would retain a living brain in a living body, erasing the neuronal patterns associated with all emergent aspects of its consciousness would utterly destroy its mind.

At the moment, downloading is technological fantasy and is likely to remain so for some time. Yet downloading is an interesting prospect for the purposes of this discussion because this quite literal transformation of human life and consciousness into a technological product extends the AI evolution-of-consciousness hypothesis to its logical conclusion. As noted earlier, a number of experts in computer science, like Robert Jastrow, John Kemeny, Marvin Minsky, and Claude Shannon, believe that consciousness, in all of its complex dimensions, will eventually exist on a different physical substrate. And we can add to this list three other names that, along with Minksy, represent the founders of artificial intelligence: Allen Newell and Herb Simon at Carnegie-Mellon, and John McCarthy at Stanford.

Joseph Weizenbaum, on the other hand, is not sympathetic with the AI evolution-of-consciousness hypothesis. As he puts it, "There's nothing left after you've destroyed the human species. Humans are the ultimate value. It's so fundamental. Everything else is based on that."[2] The problem is that defending this "ultimate value," even in the immediate technological future, may require something more than a visceral sense of its correctness. The dilemma faced by Weizenbaum is illustrated in the follow-

ing passage, in which he tries to reconcile his conviction
that human life and consciousness on their present physical substrate are the ultimate value with his informed
views on the future capabilities of AI computer systems:

> I accept the idea that a modern computer is suffi-
> ciently complex and autonomous to warrant our talk-
> ing about it as an organism. Given that it can both
> sense and affect its environment, I even grant that it
> can, in an extremely limited sense, be "socialized,"
> that is, modified by its experiences with its world. I
> grant also that a suitably constructed robot can be
> made to develop a sense of itself, that it can, for exam-
> ple, learn to distinguish between parts of itself and
> objects outside of itself, that it can be made to assign
> a higher priority to guarding its own parts against
> physical damage than to similarly guarding objects
> external to itself, and that it can form a model of
> itself which could, in some sense, be considered a kind
> of self-consciousness. When I say therefore that I am
> willing to regard such a robot as an "organism," I
> declare my willingness to consider it a kind of ani-
> mal. And I have already agreed that I see no way to
> put a bound on the degree of intelligence such an
> organism could, in principle at least, attain.[3]

Weizenbaum's informed views on what can be accomplished in the technological future lead him to the conclusion that a computer might be conscious, and that it is
difficult to establish any upper limit on the degree of intelligence this new "organism" can attain. Where, then, does
one draw the line between biologically based human consciousness and computer consciousness? The line is drawn
with an assertion of the primacy of belief over fact.
"Man," writes Weizenbaum, "is not a machine" and,
therefore, "Computers and men are not species of the same
genus."[4] That this belief is not subject, in Weizenbaum's
view, to empirical demonstration is made clear in his
frequent claim that there "are things beyond the power of
science to fully comprehend." Although accepting the pri-

macy of belief over fact may be the manner in which this question is finally resolved, advocates of the AI evolution-of-consciousness hypothesis tend to relegate such positions to the realm of personal and private conviction.

Claude Shannon, who dismisses the theist position with the simple assertion, "I see no God involved," has arrived at the conclusion that "we are basically machines but of a very complex type."[5] His views are essentially the same as those of Norbert Wiener, who earlier claimed that life is nothing more than a very complicated set of information transfers. Nils Nilsson, who heads up the AI research group at SRI International in Menlo Park, California, has also concluded that "Mind is a program." He offers the following analysis of why some of us resist the implications of this conclusion: "One's personhood feels threatened by the prospect of intelligent machines. It's a lot like what happened when Darwinian theory came along. A lot of people resisted it, because it was nicer to think otherwise. Now of lot of people are resisting artificial intelligence, I think, for the same reason."[6]

The alternate view of the character of human life and consciousness endorsed by the advocates of the AI evolution-of-consciousness hypothesis is well illustrated in Moravec's *Mind Children*. Natural or Darwinian evolution, writes Moravec, is "blind to its future" and has randomly "engineered us into a position where we can supply just a little of the vision it lacks."[7] At the moment, he says, human beings are "uncomfortable halfbreeds, part biology, part culture, with many of our biological traits out of step with our inventions."[8] Much of our reluctance to accept the inevitable movement toward the existence of consciousness on a different physical substrate is due to what Moravec terms our "body-identity position." Our problem is that we insist on associating consciousness with our bodies and, therefore, with the physical substrate of the human brain. The more enlightened view, he claims, is "pattern-identity," which defines "self" or "personhood" in terms of patterns or processes that merely happen at present to reside on a biological substrate. Mind is not, therefore, "tied to a particular body" and "not even bound to a particular pattern. It can be presented by any one of an infinite class of patterns that are equivalent only in a certain, very abstract way."[9]

According to Moravec, at the present stage in the evolution of consciousness we are coming to realize that the division between "natural" and "artificial" intelligence is not valid, and that it will "matter little in the long run whether or not humans are an intimate part of the evolving artificial intelligences."[10] This means that body-identity concerns, like "life, death, and identity," ultimately will be recognized as passing illusions occasioned by the limited state of consciousness on its present biological substrate. Since he presumes that the evolution of consciousness into existence on a nonbiological substrate is driven by the same dynamics that produced consciousness on a biological substrate, Moravec consistently describes advances in computer technologies, and the economic and political realities contributing to those advances, in terms of Darwinian evolution.

For example, computer "viruses" are characterized as "diseases" that spread through the computer population, just as biological viruses spread through the human population. "The most virulent form of software wildlife," writes Moravec, "has been called a virus—a program that, once inserted into a large program, acts to copy itself into other programs, just as a biological virus is a piece of genetic code that, once inserted into a cell, acts to copy itself into other cells."[11] Similarly, Moravec claims that the "humanlike performance" of robots has acquired, even at this early stage, "a relentless, Darwinian vigor."[12] Since Darwinian evolution is clearly at work in the evolution of computer intelligence, the best strategy is to speed the process along by "imitating the evolution of animal minds, by striving to add capabilities to machines a few at a time, so that the resulting sequence of machine behaviors resembles the capabilities of animals with increasingly complex nervous systems."[13] Moravec's understanding of natural evolution also explains why we must "rush headlong into an era of intelligent machines." The reason is simply that "societies and economies are surely as subject to competitive evolutionary pressures as are biological organisms."[14] This allegedly "self-evident" fact is demonstrated, he suggests, in the competition between cultures to secure resources in the "accessible universe."[15]

Defending the Integrity of the Wet Machine

The most ardent defense of human consciousness as different from any simulation of this consciousness on another physical substrate has been made by two philosophers, Herbert Dreyfus and John Searle.[16] One feature of Dreyfus's argument is that the limitations of the present generation of AI computers reflect fundamental technical roadblocks that simply cannot be overcome in any future technology. The inherent difficulty in this approach is illustrated by a controversy which first arose in 1965, when Arthur Samuel produced a computer program that played checkers. The program improved its skills with practice and was able to beat an American checker-playing champion. Dreyfus responded that there was a difference between the kind of computer intelligence needed to play checkers and "real" human intelligence. The program, he said, was no more a step toward human consciousness than an ape climbing a tree is a step toward the moon.

After Herbert Simon produced a chess-playing program in 1967 capable of beating a ten-year-old child, Dreyfus proclaimed that real chess, unlike checkers, could not be "truly" played by a digital computer. In this second controversy, Dreyfus was challenged to play the chess program, and, much to the delight of the advocates of the hypothesis, he lost. Undeterred, Dreyfus responded that he was a rank amateur at chess, that the demonstration proved nothing, and that computers would never be able to play "real" chess. At the core of Dreyfus's position is the belief that much that is central to human thought, like judgment, perception, and understanding, cannot be reproduced by following rules. And his primary means of defending this position is to appeal to the "authority" of philosophers, like Husserl and Heidegger, who assert that there are extrascientific or metaphysical bases for human consciousness.

The problem with Dreyfus's defense of the ineffable character of human consciousness, illustrated in the title of his book *What Computers Can't Do*, is that it grows consistently weaker with every advance in computer technologies. Although there may, in fact, be some fundamental roadblocks in the way of creating a conscious computer by the Turing criteria, one must choose them carefully and with the full awareness that they may be overcome in time. Advocates of the AI evolution-of-consciousness hypothesis also find it difficult to take Dreyfus's arguments about what computers cannot do seriously because they apply to information processing based on the top-down approach to computer design, like that of traditional Von Neumann computers. His conceptions of the limitations of "rules" do not make sense when the bottom-up approach, like that used in neural nets, is employed, and where processes like judgment, perception, and understanding could become emergent properties of a collective organization of computing elements.

The best known of Searle's arguments against the prospect of a conscious computer is the Chinese Room thought experiment. Here we are asked to imagine that there is a man inside a room in which the only entrance is a door containing a small mailbox-like slot. Although the man reads and understands English, he neither reads nor understands Chinese. Inside the room are a large number of flashcards upon which are printed Chinese characters, and a book giving instructions in English about how to process the cards through the slot. As a card is passed into the room through the slot, the man looks at the Chinese character on the card, and then refers to his instruction book where pictures of the characters appear along with a set of instructions. After he matches the character with the English instructions that indicate which cards within the room should be passed back through the slot and in what order, he follows these instructions. Although the cards being transferred into and out of the room contain meaningful information, like answering questions about recent political events, the man processing the cards knows nothing of this. Yet it could well appear on the part of people outside the room that he does understand Chinese, and is, therefore, making intelligent and conscious responses to all the questions.

What Searle is trying to illustrate is that information processing in computers, identified in the thought experiment with the man sorting the cards, is accomplished only in terms of a set of rules or in terms of syntax. There is no true intelligence or consciousness at work here, argues Searle, because semantics, or the forms in language that convey meaning in a complex relation of signs and symbols, cannot be reduced to a set of rules or to syntax alone. These assumptions then provide the basis for the following line of argumentation: (1) brains have minds; (2) minds have mental content, particularly semantic context; (3) syntax is not sufficient to constitute semantics; and (4) computer programs are entirely defined by their formal, or syntactic, structure. The conclusion is, therefore, that the computer can never in principle be conscious as human beings are conscious, because mind is an inescapable precondition for this kind of consciousness.

The most frequent rebuttal by the advocates of the AI evolution-of-consciousness hypothesis is that while the man inside the room may not understand Chinese, the entire system—consisting of the man, the flashcards, the rule book, etc.—*does* understand Chinese. The logical trick played by Searle is to place the entire system inside the brain of the man, and it is this which allows him to blur the distinction between simulation and duplication. The choice of such a strategy suggests, according to the advocates, that the philosopher is stuck in a meaningless quandary, nicely illustrated by Descartes's famous dictum "cogito, ergo sum." The underlying assumption that makes for this quandary is that wherever there is thought, there must be an "I," or agent, that informs the thinking process. Another and more recent argument used to refute Searle's position is similar to that used to refute the position taken by Dreyfus. Although semantics might be virtually impossible to emulate on computers with top-down designs or architectures, it is conceivable that semantics could be emulated on bottom-up computer designs or architectures, where the associative aspects of semantics could be an emergent phenomena. This, as we have seen, is the view taken by Lakoff.

The philosopher Karl Popper has taken a position in this debate that resembles those of Dreyfus and Searle.[17] Although he makes a sophisticated argument, his position is essentially that mind exists in a mental state outside of space-time, and that brain acts as a kind of receiver for mind. He concedes that the activity of mind can be altered by the state of the brain. Yet he also contends that one cannot conclude that mind is produced by brain. Attempts are made to validate this assumption by demonstrating that much of our mental experience, like imaginings and daydreams, will never be explained in terms of the physical substrate of the human brain. John Searle has advanced a similar argument premised on the assumption that mind is an emergent property of the material brain, and that this property cannot be explained in terms of individual material elements.[18] For example, assembled nucleotides in a DNA molecule display an emergent property that is not common to any other complex molecule: the DNA molecule can replicate itself. Just as this property of DNA is not identifiable with any physical substrate in the nucleotides, so mind, it is argued, is an emergent property of brain and cannot be reduced to brain.

The notion that mind is something other than brain is

not taken seriously, as we have repeatedly seen, by advocates of the AI evolution-of-consciousness hypothesis. For
example, Allen Newell and Herbert Simon argue that anything that transforms information or manipulates signs
must be supported by some physical substrate. They claim
that this "physical symbol system" hypothesis will play
the same role in cognitive science that hypotheses like
atoms and cells have played in physics and biology.[19]
Another notion that makes no sense to the advocates of the
AI evolution-of-consciousness hypothesis is the idea that
self or mind is an emergent property that cannot be reduced to the sum of its parts or made subject to full scientific description. For example, one could argue that an
emergent property tends in the progress of science to display itself as the same logical type as the elements from
which it emerges, or, if this is not the case, that a mathematically rigorous description of the emergent property
could lead to a different view of the elements from which it
emerges. If, for example, the physics of deterministic
chaos does serve to describe the manner in which neuronal patterns are widely distributed and redundant in the
human brain, this should lead to a different view of actual
physical processes on the level of the synapse.

Most advocates of the hypothesis are also very much
aware that the arguments posed by their detractors are
premised on extensions or refinements of Cartesian dualism. The advocates have little tolerance for those who
posit a categorical distinction between mind and matter
because any such distinction is necessarily based on a
belief in a domain of reality that can never in principle be
comprehended or described in scientific theory and experiment. Anyone who has studied the progress of modern
science knows very well that the list of phenomena previously assumed to be indescribable or unknowable in
scientific terms has grown progressively shorter. And this
leads the advocates of the hypothesis to conclude that
mind as emergent property or activity of the human brain
will also be removed from this list. For those thoroughly

inducted into the culture of scientists-engineers, it is something like heresy to presume otherwise.

Perhaps the most expedient way to appreciate the differences between how advocates of the hypothesis and their humanist–social scientist detractors deal with the mind-body problem is to appeal to a notion formulated by Kant. Kant suggested that there are at least two kinds of reason that we employ in coming to terms with reality: the "theoretical reason" of science and the "practical reason" of everyday life. Theoretical reason is a third-person perspective that seeks to comprehend all aspects of reality, including mind and consciousness, in terms of physical theories. Practical reason, in contrast, is a first-person perspective in which thoughts, feelings, loves, hopes, and desires are apprehended as self-evident truths that inform the very structure of human existence. Since living in the world in accordance with practical reason seems to provide experiential verification that the mind is autonomous and that the self is a free moral agent, practical reason easily leads one to the conclusion that mind, for practical purposes at least, is independent or separate from brain.

It is safe to assume that no human being who maintains a sane relationship to other human beings lives totally in accordance with the dictates of theoretical reason. While a neuroscientist might be able to offer a theoretical explanation for his or her love for a spouse or a child in terms of the neuronal organization and activities of the human brain, it is highly unlikely that this individual could experience or express this love in any manner that seemed authentic without appealing to practical reason. At the same time, those who are committed to the third-person perspective of theoretical reason tend to accept its truths as more primary and self-legitimating than those of practical reason. From the perspective of theoretical reason, practical reason's experiential evidence that mind and consciousness are separate from brain is an illusion foisted upon us by the emergent properties of the neuronal activities of brain. Since theoretical reason dictates that mind and consciousness are a biological-material process that will eventually become explicable in terms of natural laws, Cartesian dualism, which posits the existence of a domain of reality that is either metaphysical or extrascientific or both, is completely disallowed. What theoretical reason legitimates as a self-evident truth is that the states of mind and the states of brain are in principle identical.

The inherent weakness in the arguments developed by the humanists–social scientists in their efforts to refute the AI evolution-of-consciousness hypothesis is that they attempt to demonstrate the efficacy of the truths of practical reason within the conceptual framework of theoretical reason. The humanists–social scientists have, in effect, engaged the advocates of the hypothesis in the mind-matter debate on a conceptual turf where the rules of what constitutes valid, admissible evidence are owned and defined by the advocates. This also explains much of the confusion surrounding the debate over whether a computer that is conscious by the Turing criteria can be presumed conscious as we are conscious.

Practical reason provides experiential evidence that consciousness has an existence that is somehow anterior to or separate from the neuronal activities of brain. This suggests that any simulation of this consciousness, no matter how complete, could not possibly replicate the extrascientific dimension of consciousness. Yet for the advocates of the hypothesis there is no extrascientific dimension of consciousness—nothing lies outside of the descriptive power of physical theory and experiment. Consciousness from the third-person perspective of theoretical reason is defined in terms of the emergent properties of the information-processing system of the human brain, a system whose internal principles and dynamics will eventually be reduced to scientific description and understanding. Therefore, when a computer passes the Turing test, or when a computer displays the full range of emergent properties associated with the information-processing system of the human brain, we will have no choice but to regard this system as conscious. From this third-person perspective, it makes no difference whether the computer displays the emergent properties of consciousness on a physical substrate other than the human brain. Nor does it matter that the internal design and dynamics of this computer could be quite different from those of the human brain. If the computer manages to process its information in ways that allow it to meet any reasonably complete set of objective criteria for a conscious system, then the system, according to the advocates of the hypothesis, must be conscious.

When advocates of the AI evolution-of-consciousness hypothesis respond to arguments that make more overt appeals to metaphysics, like those that claim that the complexities of human life and consciousness are engineered by God, they typically point out that nature in the modern scientific view is not always a reliable programmer. Human diseases are now understood in terms of misinformation in the genetic program of the cell, and birth defects are rather obvious errors in programming. Any faith that one might have in the willful purpose of natural evolution, and in our biological selves as its ultimate expression, must surely be undermined, suggest the advocates, by the empirically valid conclusion that the basic mechanism of mutation involves chance reconfigurations of the DNA code. If our consciousness evolved as a result of such accidents, then we should direct the evolution of computer technology to its highest level of expression, free from the inherent indeterminacy of natural evolution.

Confronting the Second Self

What I hope to demonstrate in the concluding chapters is that the allegedly scientific premises behind the AI evolution-of-consciousness hypothesis are refutable within the framework of theoretical reason. In other words, I will try to undermine the hypothesis without making any overt appeal to extrascientific or metaphysical assumptions, and also by adhering to the logic of discourse and the rules for admissible evidence as they are defined in the scientific community. For the moment, however, let us continue to presume the correctness of the hypothesis and contemplate the terms of our evolving relationship with the emergent consciousness of computer technologies.

Psychologist Sherry Turkle suggests in *The Second Self* that thus far the terms of this relationship have provided a "new discourse for describing the divided self. On one side is placed what is simulable; on the other, that which cannot be simulated. People who say they are perfectly comfortable with the idea of mind as machine assent to the idea that simulated thinking is thinking, but often cannot bring themselves to propose further that simulated feeling is feeling."[20] What is more interesting is that Turkle has discovered that computer-literate children do not define themselves with respect to their difference from animals, but rather with respect to their difference from computers. Whereas adults might conceive of themselves as rational animals, these children tend to conceive of themselves as feeling computers. Over the next few decades more adults may become childlike in this sense, as conventional AI systems relying on script-based knowledge, heuristics, and non-monotonic logic solve complex problems, model situations, and make predictions with increased precision, accuracy, and speed. During this same time frame the ability of neural nets to form categories and make associations could become considerably more advanced, and the nets may be relied upon extensively to assess and manage a vast new range of human activities.

The new class of problems that may be faced after the neural-network revolution makes its presence fully known is illustrated by some responses made by Carl Hewitt, an artificial intelligence expert at MIT, to questions posed by Grant Fjermedal in *The Tomorrow Makers*. Hewitt has taken the position that we could achieve greater stability in the nuclear age if governments entrusted their nuclear arsenals to an independent organization of artificial intelligence robots, under the control of advanced computer systems. In such an arrangement, says Hewitt, "You are giving up something in return for some potential gains in terms of stability. And you are trusting to a certain extent that you have created this benevolent form of life that will want to keep the species around and preserve it."[21] When asked if we might better achieve this stability through human understanding, Hewitt responded:

> I think that better understanding helps. But history is not on the side of long-term human understanding. The necessary turnover in personnel you get in human-based systems, because of their very short life- times, seems to throw instability into the system. And the general diversity of human stock we have, in terms of different languages, cultures, and interests, is not something that can be smoothed over very quickly.
>
> And because of the growth of other technologies, such as nuclear technology and weapons technology, and the very rapid progress in those fields, we have a tremendous mismatch in terms of how far you can evolve the humanistic political system as opposed to the rate of advance of weaponry. So I think some kind of technology has to come in here to counterbalance and help control these other galloping technologies.[22]

Later in the conversation, Fjermedal asked how moral values could emerge in the minds of this futuristic peacekeeping force of robots. "I think," Hewitt responded, "by incorporating certain principles and processes into the operation. But beyond that, those are emergent phenomena. In other words, the humaneness of the computer system, its ability to be just, will emerge from the processes that we set up inside the machine, because we can't specify ahead of time with all that much detail and concreteness what we mean by justice."[23]

However one feels about turning over the fate of the human species to the control of a computer intelligence and its hopefully benevolent robotic peace-keeping force, Hewitt seems quite correct on one point: the "humanistic political system" has failed to adequately deal with the advance of technologies of destruction. What is most interesting is how he explains that failure. First, he argues that there is a lack of continuity resulting from the shortness of the lifespan of human managers. Second, he claims that linguistic and cultural differences correlate with different means and methods of valuation. This same dynamic also makes it highly unlikely, suggests Hewitt, that the species will survive on its own. Hewitt's hope for survival is premised, then, not on the humaneness of humankind, but rather on the humaneness of computer systems. Although the latter will "emerge" from the processes we build into the systems, the inference is that the humaneness of the computer could be quite different from, and superior to, our own humaneness in all its bewildering and conflicting formulations.

What seems terribly flawed in this analysis is the assumption that a superior humanity will spontaneously emerge in the conscious computer. By far the more probable scenario is that any emergent humanity in the conscious computer will be a more amplified version of the culturally derived and bound conception of humanity that has been programmed into the computer. Even if we assume that the computer will learn from its experience, the form and content of that experience can be no more objective than "objective" news reporting. The computer's learned experience will, in short, be a reflection of our conception of what constitutes human reality in the particular domain of the computer's expertise. The operative assumptions underlying more global computer programs that are designed to assess or evaluate the appropriateness of any action could be enfolded into subsequent programs in the generational advance of computers. If we also anticipate that the developers of such systems will follow the usual pattern of turning their attention elsewhere after the development stage is complete, then the original criteria for decision making and evaluation may be unknown and inaccessible to users of these systems.

In Search of the Human Values

If future AI systems did reflect our best sense of humanity, we could create a much more humane environment. The computer as research tool will assist us in eliminating major human diseases and should also provide the basis for understanding and reversing the damage that we are now doing to the ecosystem. This research tool might also allow us to greatly diminish hunger through better management of existing resources and more efficient production of foodstuffs in biotechnology. It also has the potential in educational applications, which we have only just begun to explore, to better combat illiteracy and ignorance, to improve the quality of education generally, and to make education a lifelong activity that is perpetually interesting. Robotics and advances in computer-assisted manufacturing systems could become the basis for a cornucopia of goods and services, which could theoretically be enjoyed by their consumers without backbreaking, or dull and repetitive, labor. The same technology might also be used to provide adequate housing for much of the world's population. And all of this could occur as the computer assists us in charting new frontiers of knowledge in space and on the frontier of complexity that is biological life.

If, however, the dynamics of group-against-group competition continue to be the prime determinant of computer applications, we can reasonably expect that our security and peace will be no more enhanced by computer technologies in the future than they have been enhanced by offensive or defensive nuclear weapons technologies in the past.

Yet one cannot help but agree with Hewitt on one point: our record of humane behavior is dismal. However, rather than give up on the prospect that our behavior can be more humane, it seems to me that we should pursue this goal with a newfound sense of its importance, and with a large awareness of why the past formulations have failed.

One vitally important realization in achieving this goal is that most of us, in my experience at least, do apparently believe that the lawful regularities of natural evolution serve on some level to explain or legitimate economic and political competition between individuals and cultures. Yet even if we assume that decisions regarding the development and use of technologies are freely made by collections of individuals in societal institutions or organizations, the record shows that we normally elect the progress that does, in fact, enhance our economic and political power. All of which could mean that we will tend to support the development and deployment of new computer technologies that might bring us incrementally closer to confirming the validity of the AI evolution-of-consciousness hypothesis, even if we happen to disagree fundamentally with its goals and assumptions. And our willingness to do so will, of course, be read by those who advance this hypothesis as confirmation of its validity.

Although I do think that we will be able to undermine the legitimacy of the AI evolution-of-consciousness hypothesis within the context of theoretical reason, this will not in itself prevent the advocates' vision of the technological future from becoming a reality. The fundamental challenge is to develop a conceptual framework that will allow us to make decisions about the uses of new AI computer technologies in ways that will serve to nurture and protect the ultimate value of human life and consciousness. It may happen, of course, that moral or religious authority within the context of particular cultures will effectively deal with the problem of valuation and protect the ultimate value within these cultures. Yet the dilemma is that social, political, and economic realities that drive competition between even very similar cultures for market share in new computer technologies is such that efforts to protect the ultimate value tend to be very weak and ineffectual. And there is the added difficulty that metaphysical assumptions featured in mythoreligious systems quite different from our own, like those appealed to by Mori in contemporary Japan, can lead to utterly opposing views on whether AI systems should be regarded as "conscious beings," or even whether they should be welcomed as our "conscious descendants."

The framework that I have in mind for evaluating the use-value of new AI technologies is based on an understanding of the character of human reality that has been widely adopted in the social sciences and massively reinforced by neuroscience. The most important aspect of this alternate framework for evaluation is that it forces us to be more aware of how we could externalize the "content" of our consciousness into the emergent consciousness of AI computer systems. Yet what I am most concerned to make clear in the remaining chapters is something that seems abundantly obvious. If we are to avoid another massive tragedy in human affairs, we must begin to exercise our philosophical and moral imaginations in ways that lead to a very different understanding of the nature of technological progress and the goals that this progress is intended to serve.

CHAPTER 7

Fundamentals of Biological Computing: A New Basis for Valuation

*Perhaps, however, Hans Moravec is right, and
man is in the process of disappearing into the
machines he has created.*
—O. B. Hardison, Jr.
Disappearing Through the Skylight

Neuroscience is in the process of disclosing the heretofore
mysterious and ineffable aspects of human consciousness
to scientific understanding. And we can reasonably anticipate that a description of all dynamic processes involved
will be relatively complete within a fifty-year time frame.
Although consciousness from the first-person perspective
of practical reason will continue to seem ineffable and
mysterious, consciousness from the third-person perspective of theoretical reason is rapidly being disclosed to
scientific understanding. As the scientific description becomes more complete, the gross, approximate, and largely
metaphoric representations of the dynamics of human consciousness that we now appeal to in both cognitive and
behavioral psychology will be displaced by an awareness
of the actual mechanisms involved. Whenever science has
managed to subsume any aspect of nature with such de-

scriptions, the general tendency among educated human beings has been to adopt a more rational and objectivist view and to abandon appeals to mythoreligious explanations. The same tendency could be displayed as science progressively discloses the underlying physical principles and dynamics of the information-processing activities of the human brain.

Meanwhile, AI systems will come into existence on a physical substrate other than the human brain that will display abilities comparable to those of the brain. Yet unlike human brains, these systems will not be limited in their cognitive abilities and in the scope of relevant data available for analysis by a set number of processing units, connections, and so on. We can, therefore, reasonably anticipate that they will become faster and better than human intelligence in analyzing and solving complex problems in dedicated applications. Presuming that these systems also eventually display self-reflective awareness with full emotional coloration, we may elect to confer a sense of "self" upon them. Even Joseph Weizenbaum, the AI theorist who appears most sensitive to the threats advancing AI computer systems pose to the value of human life and consciousness, has declared himself willing to confer a sense of "self" on future AI systems, and even to regard them as "organisms," or as a species of intelligent life.

Part of what I mean to demonstrate in the remainder of this book is that if progress in AI computer technologies continues to confirm the vision of the future advanced by the advocates of the AI evolution-of-consciousness hypothesis, it will not be because we had no choice in the matter. The naive scientific legitimation of the hypothesis, which argues that the laws of Darwinian evolution are compelling consciousness into existence on a nonbiological substrate, is quite absurd from a scientific point of view. If we perceive any lawful regularities in economic and political reality that seem to be legislating over decisions about the development of new AI technologies, it is only because we conceive of them as such in our subjective realities and behave accordingly. Also, our present understanding of the dynamics of Darwinian evolution indicates that evolution does not and cannot operate on inorganic matter. Although it is not difficult to undermine this naive attempt to legitimate the scientific validity of the hypothesis, there is a more sophisticated scientifically based legitimation that I will confront and attempt to undermine in the concluding chapter.

Even if we do manage to undermine all efforts to legitimate the AI evolution-of-consciousness hypothesis in scientific terms, this will not even begin to speak to our primary dilemma. How do we make decisions about the development and deployment of new AI technologies in a manner that serves to maintain our economic well-being and geopolitical power, and yet manage at the same time to nurture and protect the ultimate value of human life and consciousness? My position is that if we continue to assume that the former is necessarily congruent with the latter, we should be prepared to accept the proposition that the transformation of human life and consciousness into technological products may be inevitable.

Human Brain as Information-Processing System

For those of us committed to serving the ultimate value, the obvious challenge is to develop an alternate framework for assessing the use-value of new technologies that effectively serves this value. The framework developed here is premised on an understanding of the character of human reality that has existed for some time in the social sciences and that has been massively reinforced by neuroscience. Those who attempt to articulate this new understanding of the special character of human reality typically begin by pointing out that the "true" or real world for other species is principally a function of the neuronal organization of their brains. Although many mammals can learn and transmit new behaviors within their social group, the vast majority of behaviors for all nonhuman species is the direct or indirect result of genetic programming. Yet in the case of our own species, there is no convincing evidence that genetic programming exercises any direct control over any specific social behavior, or that it legislates over any aspect of the shape or content of human reality transculturally.

This does not mean that culture replaces genetic evolution, or that genetically controlled predispositions play no role in human behavior. Genetic research has produced substantial evidence of hereditary variation in color vision, hearing acuity, odor and taste discrimination, number and spatial ability, memory, perceptual skill, spelling, sentence construction, psychomotor skill, and timing of major stages in intellectual development and language acquisition. There is also evidence suggesting that hereditary variation might predispose individuals to phobias, alcoholism, homosexuality, and certain forms of neurosis and psychosis, including manic-depressive behavior and schizophrenia.[1] Yet genetic inheritance does not provide a template for a specific range of human behaviors or deterministically program any complex set of such behaviors. The majority scientific view is represented by figures like Stephen Jay Gould. His position is that although scientific studies on correlations between genetically programmed neuronal organization and human behavior do force us to recognize the role of "biological potential," they do not in the least argue for "biological determinism."[2]

In our species preadaptive evolutionary conditions allowed for the invention and refinement of the symbol system of spoken language, and thereby enabled us to create and transmit human culture. Although these linguistic and cultural software programs were running on similar hardware, the hardware apparently placed few constraints on the variability of these programs. Consequently, transformations in both human environments and the experience of ourselves in those environments occurred at a rate much in excess of the normal course of

Darwinian evolution. Since we also were able to external-ize subjectively based human ideas or constructs as tools, clothing, shelter, etc., we came to live in a non-species-specific environment, or in an environment where sur-vival was not utterly dependent on hardwired responses to specific environmental stimuli or conditions.

Recent studies in neuroscience indicate that even those of us who have assimilated virtually the same linguistic and cultural programs and have virtually the same life experiences cannot be assumed to construct highly identi-cal realities. Comparisons of the brains of siblings—even those of identical twins—during a postmortem reveal gross differences in morphology and staggering varia-tions in cell-to-cell organization. Although all healthy individuals have similar brain structures, the proportion of cells in each of these structures and the manner in which they interconnect are unique to the individual. As the neuroscientist Vernon Mountcastle puts it, "Each of us lives within the universe—the prison—of his own brain. Projecting from it are millions of fragile sensory nerve fibers, in groups, uniquely adapted to sample the energetic states of the world around us: heat, light, force, and chem-ical compositions. This is all we know directly: all else is logical inference"[3] (see Figure 14).

What I am suggesting is that the history of human consciousness, as that story is told by science and the social sciences, suggests that the tendency of cognitive scientists to compare the human brain with hardware and linguistic and cultural systems with software is neither trivial nor inappropriate. Human beings are programmed in a manner analogous to programming computers. The hardware that is our brain allows us to assimilate the software of language, and this software becomes the basis for encoding all aspects of the elaborate software package of a transmitted culture. The hardware happened in the course of its evolutionary history to develop enough excess neuronal capacity and alternate neuronal organization to run this software. Subsequent improvements in hardware

Figure 14 Schizophrenia in Monozygotic Twins

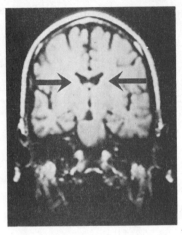 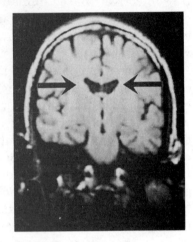

Unaffected   **Affected**

Loss of brain volume associated with schizophrenia is clearly shown by magnetic resonance imaging (MRI) scans comparing the sizes of the ventricles (butterfly shaped, fluid-filled spaces in the midbrain) of identical forty-four-year-old male twins, one of whom has schizophrenia (right). The ventricles of the person with schizophreia are larger than his twin's.

capacity and internal organization allowed for increased levels of sophistication in the range and complexity of the software programs. These two developments, in concert, provided a clearer evolutionary advantage.

The analogy is not, of course, exact. Self-progamming computers do not as yet exist, and the structure of linguistic and cultural programs is quite different from, and apparently far more complex than, present computer programs. More important, the human brain is adaptive and context-dependent, and it has enormous generalizing powers. Also, prior to linguistic and cultural programming, the human brain is not, like a conventional computer prior to programming, a tabula rasa, or blank slate. The biological potentials that accrued in our evolutionary history evolved prior to the programming effort and condition its success. Yet the analogy is useful in contemplating how the history of human consciousness allows us to better understand the character of human reality, and the role that new technologies might play in altering the structure of that reality.

The Evolution of the Wet Machine

The evolutionary success of our species is commonly explained in terms of our larger brain size or, more accurately, the so-called encephalization quotient: brain size relative to body weight. But this in itself would not have guaranteed our survival, and certainly not in such impressive numbers. Brain size is a functional adaptation to environmental conditions, and not a quantity with an inherent tendency to increase. For most of the 150 million years of mammalian life the basic mammalian brain did not expand. Environmental conditions that made an enlarged brain a more efficient way of perpetuating life forms apparently arose some sixty-five million years ago, during the period in which the dinosaurs became extinct. Our own brain is an evolutionary extension of a pattern that began some seventy-five million years ago with small, tree-dwelling mammals similar to rats and shrews. Current speculation is that we shared our last common ancestor with gorillas and chimps about six million years ago at most. Yet brain size as a preadaptive condition did became an evolutionary advantage at the point at which the excess neuronal capacity allowed us to invent a new tool that proved remarkably useful in the quest for survival.

Although we will never know the exact encephalization quotient that made this invention possible, some anthropologists have speculated that the process began when the brain size of *Homo habilis* grew to roughly 600–800 cm^3 some three million years ago.[4] Homo habilis may have been the first of our ancestors with enough excess neuronal organization, or hardware, to invent the first rudimentary elements of spoken language. Subsequent refinements of this tool, in concert with increased neuronal capacity, would eventually make *Homo habilis*'s descendants an evolutionary success par excellence. During the million-year transition from *Homo habilis* to *erectus*, the neocortex, which became the principal center for association and thought, more than doubled in size. Although tracings in fossil skulls provide only very indirect evidence of architectural changes, such changes were obviously quite profound. Based on careful and extensive studies of correlations between increased brain size in hominids and the emergence of language and culture, Philip Tobias evolved the following formulae: "increase in brain size = gain in neuronal organization = rise in complexity of nervous function = even more diversified and complicated behavioral responses = progressively amplified and enhanced cultural manifestations."[5]

Although the evolution of *erectus* was rapid in comparison with most other organisms, it was glacially slow in comparison with the rate at which *Homo sapiens* emerged from the Paleolithic era and evolved into *Homo sapiens sapiens* about one hundred thousand years ago. The enlarged brain of *Homo sapiens sapiens*, coupled with increasingly more sophisticated language systems, manifested its power to coordinate experience primarily through more elaborate social organization. Fossil records suggest that there was a dramatic evolution of the material culture of *Homo sapiens sapiens* beginning some forty thousand years ago. Even representational art appears at this time, in the form of clay and stone sculpture along with simple but strikingly beautiful cave paintings. There is also the suggestion some thirty-two thousand years ago in Europe of a form of literacy, consisting of scratches or ornaments on pieces of bone, clay, and stones. The scratches appear to be arranged in repeated motifs into descriptive classes such as fishlike images, meanders, and parallel lines. Fossil records also indicate that the beginnings of the artistic phase correlated with an unusually rapid growth and expansion of human populations in the

Northern Hemisphere. At this point the ability to better coordinate experience with language and culture was proving a clear evolutionary advantage.[6]

The Development of Linguistic Software

Language as the basis for symbolic thinking, and the deepening of long-term memory to store vaster amounts of information were, then, the ultimate products of the evolution of *Homo sapiens sapiens*. In the initial stage of development language was probably a crude system of signs that overlaid the bestial sounds and gestures of the ancestral prehumans. At this early stage language is thought to have been iconic, or imitative of objects or actions that were intended or desired. Some modern linguists are convinced that language in the full sense—an arbitrary system of sound symbols that has meaning for a particular linguistic community—emerged only about fifty thousand years ago. This would serve to explain why art and the rapid evolution of materials-based culture appear at the same time.[7] The evolution of modern language systems has been traced by linguists through the Indo-European family of languages back to the ancestral, proto-Indo-European tongue spoken in the third millennium B.C.

When environmental conditions at the end of the last ice age favored sedentary food production over nomadic hunting and gathering, language and culture became the basis for larger and more complex societal organizations. The presence of trade items and status burials in hunter and gatherer tribes prior to this point suggests that more complex and hierarchical societal organizations were already evolving before the earth's climate made these skills more negotiable. The agricultural revolution began ten thousand years ago in the arc of fertile land running through present-day Israel, Jordan, Syria, Turkey, Iran, and Iraq; another similar center appeared in China seven thousand years ago.

If we measure evolutionary success in numbers of surviving species, our prehistoric ancestors were not terribly successful. The growth curve prior to ten thousand years ago, when roughly five to ten million members of our species existed, is almost flat. Then we witness a gradual increase that becomes increasingly more dramatic over the last few hundred years to reach the present figure of 5.3 billion. It is clear that this would not have occurred if the only contributing factors were survivalistic drives and physical prowess. Hardware, or the uncultivated brain that is our evolutionary inheritance, does not in itself produce an organism suited for survival, or even one that is distinctly human. The qualities that we recognize as distinctly human begin to develop only after children assimilate linguistic and cultural programs. At this point an inheritance built upon, but quite different from, innate genetic determinants and predispositions takes over. The emergent human being seems to enter a reality bounded but not dictated by its large and complex neuronal organization. As the anthropologist Clifford Geertz describes the process:

> Culture, rather than being added to a virtually finished animal, was a central ingredient in the production of that animal itself. . . . The perfection of tools, the adoption of organized hunting and gathering practices, the beginnings of true family organization, the discovery of fire, and most critically, the increasing reliance upon systems of significant symbols (language, art, myth, ritual) for orientation, communication, and self-control all created a new environment . . . by submitting himself to governance by symbolically mediated programs . . . man determined, if unwittingly, his own biological destiny. He literally created himself.[8]

Human Reality and Software Programming

Although none of us choose our native language and culture, the shape of our reality is primarily determined by both. The notion that there are universals in linguistic systems correlating with innate patterns of organization in the human brain has not been supported by research in neuroscience. But it is widely accepted that the deep structure of the linguistic program we happen to assimilate, which applies principally to the logical structure of grammar and syntax, largely determines our modes of observation and interpretation. For example, contemporary linguists are quick to point out that there are no "matters of fact" outside language because "fact" always has linguistic content. One obvious example is that if a Navaho speaker uses the equivalent of our word *blue*, we cannot presume that the reference is to the same color—one word in Navaho refers to both blue and green. This is true in spite of the fact that the hardware of the human brain predisposes normally sighted individuals to perceive variation in wavelength not as a continuously varying property of light but rather as the four basic colors of blue, green, yellow, and red. As the philosopher Wittgenstein observed, "If we spoke a different language, we would perceive a somewhat different world."⁹ Even the most casual student of anthropology can appreciate the enormous variation in the form of human reality that results when linguistic programming is overlaid with that of a cultural inheritance.

An examination of sexual mores in different cultures easily demonstrates the extent to which culture shapes human reality. While incest taboos are present in a large number of cultures, there are cultures in which incest is fully accepted. Marriage appears in such a staggering array of different patterns, as a function of societal organization and mythoreligious heritage, that the only common denominator appears to be sexual intercourse. What is deemed "normal" behavior in any given culture can be found to be "abnormal" in another. As the anthropologist Ruth Benedict observes, "It does not matter what kind of 'abnormality' we choose for illustration, those which indicate extreme instability, or those which are more on the order of character traits like sadism, or delusions of grandeur and persecution, there are well-described cultures in which these individuals function at ease and with honor."[10]

The same variability can be found in fundamental assumptions about substance, identity, and relation. Space that is regarded by members of one culture as empty can be regarded by members of another as full. The notion of self, which is conceived in much of the Western world as "skin encapsulated ego," is formulated elsewhere as a dynamic integral function of the seamless interplay of spiritual forces. Objects perceived as alike or similar in one cultural context will be perceived as categorically different in another. The world as we are programmed to conceive it is very much the world as we perceive it.

The Left Brain Verbal-Processing System

In terms of the theory of brain organization and function advanced by Gazzaniga and others, the hardware component of the brain that plays the primary role in processing linguistic and cultural software (in those of us with normal hemispheric dominance) is the left brain verbal-processing system. After this system had fully evolved, our species was able to make computations that resulted in abstract inference and to interpret a multiple self that could act based on something more than simple reflex reactions to awards and punishments. The neuronal patterns in the brain associated with the left hemisphere seem aware of inputs from other independent processing systems in the brain, and they appear dedicated to maintaining a sense of consistency in all behaviors, by interpreting overt behaviors and covert emotional responses from other brain areas. Although some neuronal patterns operate independently of the verbal-processing system, it is the inference-making capacities of this system that seem largely responsible for grasping relations between conscious inputs. What we normally term the ineffable and mysterious in our experience of self is understood as the left brain verbal-processing system's response to inputs from other systems that it either cannot translate into its structural representations of reality or that it cannot rationalize to make consistent with those representations.

One useful way to contemplate the character of the reality that the left brain verbal-processing system seeks to make consistent is to appeal to a discipline known as the sociology of knowledge. According to this discipline, in the complex interplay between inputs from other brain systems experienced in subjective reality and the demands and expectations associated with socially constructed reality, the left brain verbal-processing system eventually channels its outputs into multiple versions of reality. Among these multiple realities, the reality that presents itself as reality par excellence is the "reality of everyday life." The primary temporal dimension of this reality is time-present, and it is reinforced and legitimated by an ongoing sense of correspondence between shared meanings, normally referred to as common sense. Common-sense knowledge is the "knowledge we share with others in the normal, self-evident routines of everyday life."[11] Other realities, in relation to that of everyday life, are experienced as finite provinces of meaning—or enclaves within the paramount reality—circumscribed by different meanings and modes of experience.

The two major phases in the assimilation of social reality, according to students of the sociology of knowledge, are *primary socialization* in childhood, which leads to induction into society, and *secondary socialization*, the period in which the already socialized individual is inducted into new sectors of society. During primary socialization the dynamic neuronal patterns associated with the conscious self seem to be a reflected entity. In other words, the roles and attitudes of others are encoded through the process of identification. The social world is reflected in those with whom we closely identify and is incorporated into the neuronal patterns that allow us to construct a conscious experience of self. As we learn to construct it in this phase, reality is normally apprehended as "reality-in-itself," or as the self-evident truth about the way things are. Underlying this whole process is the left brain verbal-processing system's ability to objectify experience and to build relevance schemas on increasingly higher levels of abstraction.

Where the process of institutionalization is less than successful within the family, other control mechanisms and institutions, like civil or religious law, are required. The institutional world will eventually be apprehended by the child as an objective reality that antedates his or her birth. It is embodied in the experience of the individual through the performance of roles. The result is that the individual can reflect upon his or her biography as a whole, and discrete actions become related parts with meanings that are socially articulated and shared. In order for the process of institutionalization to be successful, the left brain verbal-processing system must eventually assimilate into its inference-making neuronal patterns beliefs and associated values.

In the initial stages the child is exposed to beliefs and values in terms of behavioral expectations and demands tied to a system of rewards and punishments. Yet a normal child will eventually arrive at a stage in its cognitive development when its inference-making left brain verbal-processing system goes beyond the level of behavioral expectations and demands. The child then requires more global explanations to maintain a sense of coherence. The function of beliefs is to provide these higher-level or more abstract explanations, and beliefs serve within the context of a mythoreligious heritage to legitimate values.

The primary function of values is to maintain the institutional order by assigning to certain attitudes and behaviors a more compelling and self-legitimating character. The one feature of this process that is terribly important to recognize and understand is reification. This fundamental dynamic of the inference-making system assigns nonhuman sources to the products of human activity. Legitimating some aspect of human behavior as a law of nature, or as a manifestation of divine will, are examples of reification. The curious effect of reification is that human beings, who are the creators and producers of their world, come to apprehend themselves as products of the world they created, thus constructing a reality that in some sense denies their selves.

A successful programming effort leads to a quite dramatic result: the creation of a symbolic universe. A symbolic universe is the ultimate achievement of the coherence-making left brain verbal-processing system, in that it serves to integrate different provinces of meaning and to encompass the institutional order in its symbolic totality. It is an all-embracing frame of reference, or a global program. Since all human experience can be seen as taking place within it, it is a universe in a very real sense. The symbolic universe tends to encompass the entire historic society and the biography of the individual, and it defines institutional roles as modes of participation in a world that transcends and includes the institutional order. Yet the left brain verbal-processing system cannot, of course, be viewed as solely responsible for either developing or sustaining a symbolic universe. Its primary function is to integrate the diverse inputs from other brain systems, such as the limbic system, which provides the emotional coloration associated with strongly held beliefs, attitudes, and convictions.

A New Basis for Evaluation

If the benefits of the technological future we have now entered are to be maximized, and the damage to the prime value minimized, our focus should not be on what computers can or cannot do. It should rather be on the manner in which we have been programmed by our own linguistic and cultural heritage and by our evolving experience in all aspects of human reality. What is perhaps most important in this study is the recognition that reified constructs are fundamental to the organization of any symbolic universe and quite resistant to change. If we are to properly consider the use-value of reified constructs in the goal-directed mechanisms of future AI systems, we must first disclose their existence to ourselves and thereby cease to reify them.

The study of the origins and history of human consciousness as that story is told by science and the social sciences also provides a very different framework for the evaluation of the impact of new technologies on human nature and identity. If we are to enlarge the framework of evaluation to contemplate potential impacts on all domains of reality that might be occasioned by new technologies, it seems clear that we must have an active and informed awareness of the subjective character of human reality and the manner in which we externalize culturally derived conceptions of this reality into computer systems. Vital to the success of this enterprise will be the realization that reification, regardless of the sense of security it provides, is no longer an affordable indulgence. What any assessment of the use-value of new technologies requires is a studied disregard for all totalizing solutions, or legitimations, and an insistence on evaluating the entire range of transformations that might be wrought by new technologies in our symbolic universe.

When we have carefully and systematically evaluated the impacts of a new technology in the past, the primary focus has tended to be on perceived advantages in economic and geopolitical terms. No matter how objective this analysis might appear in terms of the data collected and the statistical profiles used, reification normally plays a role in arriving at and interpreting the meaning of results. Reification in this area assumes many guises, ranging from powerful convictions about what all people are and need, to conceptions of the actual or "real" character of economic laws, to appeals to the will of God.

Although we may owe our ability to construct a symbolic

universe to prior events in nature that students of biology and physics have yet to fully comprehend, human ingenuity and effort deserve a great deal of credit. It is quite impossible to explain in purely Darwinian terms our survival in such impressive numbers or the myriad aspects of human cultures that have no strictly survivalistic value. The compulsion of life forms to perpetuate their genes is not a sufficient cause to explain these results. Virtually everything we value as human beings was a human creation, including the values themselves. And the same applies to scientific knowledge and to any technologies that this knowledge allows us to create. The assumption that these accomplishments are the direct result of the forces of Darwinian evolution is merely another example of reification.

An improved and active understanding of the subjective character of human reality also provides a new basis for appreciating the importance of values in maintaining cultural coherence in the interests of survival. Granted, values have often served to legitimate oppressive social orders and ritualized aggression. Yet it is also true that values, as they have evolved in the moral imaginations of the most respected figures in virtually any mythoreligious heritage one can name, have tended to affirm human life and consciousness as the ultimate value. One can, of course, view this tendency in purely empirical terms, and assume that it is merely an attempt by the left brain verbal-processing systems of particular individuals to establish greater degrees of coherence in their symbolic universe. Yet this does not obviate the fact that when the most intelligent, sensitive, and aware human beings have extended the inference-making capacity of their own world-constructing minds to the ultimate limits, the ultimate value seems almost inevitably to emerge.

Notes on the Evolution of Human Consciousness

Marshal McLuhan forecast some twenty-five years ago that the emergent global telecommunications system was, in effect, an extension of the human nervous system and would transform human consciousness in such a way as to create the sense that we live in a "global village." Distances that had previously been experienced as formidable in space and time would, he predicted, greatly contract as the new telecommunications system made us forcibly aware, at the speed of light, of the activities of other people and cultures on planet Earth. Although McLuhan's optimistic forecast was warmly embraced initially by many social theorists and analysts, it soon began to appear as rather naive as nation-states continued to engage one another in both cold and hot wars and used the new telecommunications system as an effective means of fighting such wars. Recent geopolitical developments suggest, however, that McLuhan's forecast may not have been as naive as many of us have supposed.

The construct of a nation-state, with its own language and culture and maintained by a government that expresses the "national" will, traditions, and interests is a fairly recent invention. That construct emerged as a primary feature of the symbolic universe of the inhabitants of the Western world during the sixteenth and seventeenth centuries, and the process was not complete until toward the middle of the eighteenth century. Peter Drucker was among the first political scientists to realize that social, political, and economic conditions in the modern electronic age were such that the nation-state, which had historically claimed unqualified sovereignty, could not remain the self-sustaining political unit that it has been over the last few centuries. Our new situation demands, he suggests in *Landmarks for Tomorrow*, the creation of new and more flexible institutions that overlie national boundaries and serve transnational social and economic needs.[12]

Dogmatic nationalism, which appeals to reification in the form of sacred legitimations for the existence or expansion of the sovereign nation-state, is, of course, still practiced by groups like the Sikhs of India, the Tamils of Sri Lanka, and the Shiites of Iran. Yet it seems obvious that reifications of this sort no longer have the self-legitimating character that they did even in the nineteenth century, and that most citizens of industrialized nations seem to view them as dangerously outmoded constructs.

Many commentators in the United States have, of course, appealed to reification to explain recent events in countries such as Germany, Poland, Czechoslovakia, and Romania. What tends to be reified by these commentators are "freedom," "democracy," and a "free-market economy" as lawlike regularities in human nature that are inexorably driving the institutional frameworks of other cultures into something like a carbon copy of our own. The more reasonable explanation is that reification's role in the legitimation of ideologies appears to have greatly diminished, and leaders such as Gorbachev are more willing to allow institutional reorganization where it serves to diminish conflict and enhance economic benefits.

Yet it is also clear that reification remains a fundamental dynamic in geopolitical life. For example, it appears alive and well in the ethnic nationalism that has re-emerged in Europe and the Soviet republics and is likely to be the most destabilizing force in the new world order. But the leaders of these Eastern European nation-states, and even the leaders of the Soviet republics now seeking more autonomy in their relationship to the crumbling centralized government in Moscow, clearly do not conceive of the nation-state as sovereign in the old terms. The rhetoric of such leaders almost invariably features a theme of trans-nationalism that takes the form of concerns about the removal of international trade barriers and restrictions, the availability of foreign investment, membership in transnational organizations such as the European Common Market, and links to the global telecommunications system.

However regressive the resurgence of ethnic nationalism might be, we do seem to be in the process of reprogramming our symbolic universe in ways that are leading to a growing sense that we live in a global village. And this would not have occurred in the absence of the global tele-communications revolution. On the most obvious level, when an anchorperson on the evening news reports live from cities such as Moscow or Beijing, or when man-in-the-street interviews are televised from such places, the proximity of these peoples and cultures in space and time is hard to ignore. The willingness of leaders to allow such broadcasts is also explainable at least partly in terms of the revolution in modern telecommunications.

We now live in a world in which events such as the student revolt in China or the nuclear accident at Chernobyl simply cannot be kept secret by nation-states. The electronic web of the global telecommunications system makes it enormously difficult to isolate events of even marginal geopolitical import. The relative health of any national economy is increasingly measured in terms of information that is resident in the global telecommunications network on computer systems. These systems calculate balance-of-trade figures, the relative value of currencies, the transnational flow of any goods, commodities, and services, and so on. The construct of a sovereign nation-state isolated in space and time has become outmoded.

The growing sense that we live in a global village could also lead to the recognition that progress for its own sake also involves an appeal to reification. Disclosing the role that reification plays in our understanding of the nature of technological progress could be extremely important, due to fact that we appear to be in the process of restructuring the American computer industry in response to competition from the Japanese computer industry. The construct of progress for its own sake dates from the nineteenth century, when the visionary builders of railroads, steam engines, and the production-line system in factories laid the foundations for the fossil-fueled industrial economy that now threatens to do irreparable damage to the ecosystem. It was during this same era that the American Dream, as originally formulated by figures like Benjamin

Franklin and Horatio Alger, became a good deal more than achieving a relatively modest amount of wealth and economic security through hard work and careful planning. The new formulation of the dream took the form of superman as entrepreneur, and its primary exemplars in the initial phase were figures like Jay Gould, James Fisk, Andrew Carnegie, John D. Rockefeller, Henry Ford, and Thomas Edison. A new class of such heroes would later emerge during the modern electronics revolution—represented by individuals like Tom Watson, Robert Noyce, Noland Bushnell, Steve Wozniak, and Steven Jobs.

What this particular reading of the American Dream tends to disguise, as Dick Hanson illustrates in *The New Alchemists*, is that although entrepreneurs in the computer industry have played a vitally important role and have also on occasion enjoyed more than a modest amount of financial success, the majority of the advances have resulted from competition between large computer firms.[13] What appears to be changing the competition between American computer firms is a phenomenon which insiders in the computer industry refer to as "Japan Inc." In Japan, the competition between large computer firms has differed from that between American computer firms, due to the presence of government-sponsored and financed entities like the Ministry of International Trade and Industry (MITI). When, for example, Japan began its VLSI project in the 1970s, a joint venture with a 40-60 split was established between MITI and five major firms: Hitachi, Fujitsu, Mitsubishi, Nippon, and Toshiba. MITI also provided additional assistance to these firms in the form of tax breaks, attractive bank loans, and accelerated depreciation rules. The arrangement was designed to make Japan dominant in a base technology, the semiconductor market, and it worked beautifully. And many similar arrangements have been made, as we have seen, between MITI and major Japanese manufacturers in the competition to develop the most cost-effective and efficient fifth-generation of computers.

Many industry analysts are convinced that roughly thirty major American computer companies as a loosely confederated system are not equipped to compete with the sovereign nation of Japan. Using government subsidies as an assured source of capital, major Japanese computer companies have been able to rapidly develop and manufacture new generations of chips, to accept much thinner profit margins—if not to actually tolerate losses in the initial marketing phase—and to more readily establish economies of scale in the manufacture and sale of base technologies. However, if the analysts are correct, then it is quite conceivable, as a number of recent proposals in the U.S. Congress suggest, that we may soon witness the emergence of something like "American Computer Inc." as a more effective means of competing with Japan Inc. What is troubling about this development is that if the American computer industry and the sovereign nation-state are more closely linked to one another in terms of their institutional frameworks, then we are also likely to reify any progress that is made in the industry.

If, however, we realize that the sovereign nation-state is an outmoded construct in the modern electronic era, or, more important, if we cease to reify this construct in either religious or ideological terms, then we might also realize that a belief in the inevitability of technological progress for its own sake also involves an appeal to reification. Yet success in this particular enterprise also requires us to profoundly revise our understanding of the character of economic reality. We must first realize that so-called economic laws are not "lawful" in the sense that the laws of physics are lawful. As many scholars have demonstrated, this view of the laws of economics was derived from classical physics, legitimated by an appeal to the authority of classical physics, and has been thoroughly undermined by modern physics. In our present situation the so-called laws of economic theory merely describe tendencies that can be finally understood only in terms of the motivational and attitudinal structures existing in the symbolic universe of collections of individuals.

What may eventually be required is an economic theory based on an understanding of the "ecology of institutions," as well as a pricing structure indexed against the relative damage done to the ecosystem in the production of particular goods and commodities. It is possible, for example, to conceive of an economic theory based on the understanding of entropy in modern physics. Such an economic theory would establish the costs of anything produced in terms of the amount of entropy, or disorder, that is created in the ecosystem as a consequence of production. If the entropy quotient in the production and distribution of a commodity or service is high, then its price would be higher and vice versa. If such a scheme were to evolve, advanced AI computer systems that could realisticially model the entire ecosystem and the potential damage that might be done to this system by any large-scale human activity would obviously be required.

Charles Darwin and the AI Evolution-of-Consciousness Hypothesis

What all of the above suggests is that two of the primary assumptions made by the advocates of the AI evolution-of-consciousness hypothesis seem in accord with the scientific evidence: (1) the shape of human reality is governed primarily by the linguistic and cultural software that we happen to assimilate; and (2) the character of this reality may ultimately be understood in terms of the interplay between hardware, or the dynamic patterns associated with the neuronal organization of the human brain, and software, the linguistic and cultural programs that run on this hardware. Some advocates of the hypothesis are easily proven wrong in scientific terms, however, due to a naive understanding of the manner in which natural selection works. It is this naive misunderstanding of the dynamics of evolution that also accounts for these advocates' tendency to presume that the struggle for survival mandated by natural selection is evinced in economic and political forces that are driving consciousness into existence on a different physical substrate.

Part of the confusion here is that Darwin in his original theory did suggest that economic and political forces are conditioned by the dynamics of natural selection. But he did not derive this conclusion from the data in his voluminous scientific notebooks. As the biologist Garrett Hardin has demonstrated, Darwin "introjected into the scientific world view the cybernetic scheme that pervaded the economic thinking in which he grew to manhood."[14] This scheme can be seen at work in the infamous "Essay on the Principle of Population" by Thomas Malthus, and in the writings of Herbert Spencer, the reigning champion during Darwin's lifetime of laissez-faire capitalism and rugged individualism. It was from Malthus that Darwin derived the notion of "struggle for survival," and the term itself, which appeared in the second edition of *Origin*, comes directly from Spencer. The critic Stanley Hyman, in his careful study of Darwin's prose, notes that the "archetypal image in the *Origin* is the war of nature" and arrives at the conclusion that "the dramatic and tragic vision of life comes from Darwin, rather than from his subject matter, when we see how undramatic present-day formulations of natural selections are."[15]

The disappearance of characterizations of natural selection as an open-ended struggle for survival is not a consequence of any change in political or economic philosophy. It derives from an improved understanding of the actual character of evolution. We are now aware, as Darwin could not be, of the cooperative aspects of bodily organization, of the harmonic interplay of all biological systems, and, in general, of the enormous interdependence of biological processes. Also, the notion of an organism as a discrete entity has no more place or function in modern biology than the notion of substance as a discrete entity has in modern physics. The attempt by Moravec and others to legitimate the inexorable movement toward the existence of consciousness on a different physical substrate may make sense in terms of Darwin's original theory. But it does not make sense in terms of our present understanding of the actual dynamics of natural selection.

The assumption that natural selection can be seen at work in the evolution of consciousness on a nonorganic substrate also fails to recognize something quite fundamental about the role of genes. As Stephen Jay Gould puts it, natural selection "cannot see genes and pick among them directly. It must use bodies as an intermediary. A gene is a bit of DNA hidden within a cell. . . . Hundreds of genes contribute to the building of most body parts and their action is channeled through a kaleidoscopic series of environmental influences: embryonic and postnatal, internal and external. Parts are not transparent genes, and selection doesn't work directly on parts. It accepts or rejects entire organisms because suites of parts, interacting in complex ways, confer advantages."[16]

What Gould is demonstrating is that evolution requires organic life forms that are selected in the interplay with other such forms in an ecological niche. There is no suggestion whatsoever in the scientific evidence to support the assumption by some AI theorists that Darwinian evolution necessarily drives organisms toward higher levels of complexity. That hypothesis, orginally formulated by Lamarck and others, was disproven by Darwin himself. Such misunderstandings of the character of natural selection seem to arise, as Gould points out, "from some bad habits of Western scientific thought—from attitudes . . . that we call atomism, reductionism, and determinism. The idea that wholes should be understood by decomposition into 'basic' units; that properties of miscroscopic units can generate and explain the behavior of macroscopic results; that all events and objects have definite, predictable, determined causes."[17]

When any of us assume that forces in economic and political reality are analogous to those that operate in natural selection, we are essentially making the same mistake originally made by Darwin. We are unwittingly allowing constructs arbitrarily invented by our cultural forebears in economic and political reality to cloud our understanding of scientific truths. If we are being driven to the point at which consciousness will reside on a nonbiological substrate, it is our conception of the character of social, economic, and political reality that is doing the driving.

The dynamics of evolution have provided us with a much improved understanding of how the physical substrate of the human brain evolved to the point at which the invention of language and culture became possible. But from that point onward, as Gould puts it, there were "enough neuronal connections to convert an inflexible and rather rigidly programmed device into a liable organ, endowed with sufficient logic and memory to substitute nonprogrammed learning for the direct specification as the ground for social behaviors."[18] If any aspect of social reality is programmed, it is human beings who are the programmers, and human beings who can freely elect to do any re-programming. As Simone de Beauvoir put it, "We are the being whose essence lies in having no essence."

If there is one thing that I would hope to convey in this portion of the discussion, it is this: our technological prowess has brought us to the point at which we must seriously reexamine and reassert the value of human life and consciousness, with the clear understanding that the fullness of time is too long to wait for a more widely shared sense of this value. If we continue to believe or operate as if technological progress is our ultimate value, we should not assume that this progress will perpetually enhance our sense of security, material comfort, and psychological well-being. We should assume rather that the fundamental project of technology is simply more technology, and we should be prepared to live in a world in which the value of human life and consciousness is increasingly determined by a technological future over which we have increasingly less control.

A New Basis for Dialogue Between
the Two Cultures

The time has clearly come, it seems to me, for members of the cultures of scientists-engineers and humanists–social scientists to realize that neither culture is capable of unilaterally making meaningful decisions about the proper uses of new AI technologies. The primary business at hand is to fashion a technological future in which we could effectively learn to coordinate human experience in the interests of survival, and to alleviate, if not eliminate, the terrible discrepancies between the conditions for human existence that presently exist on this planet. What seems to have been lost or displaced in the current debate over the technological future is that technology, particularly computer technologies, does have the potential to make this seemingly impossible dream possible.

For those who remain unconvinced of the importance of this dialogue, allow me to share a more complete version of the statement made by J. Doyne Farmer that was quoted in part in Chapter 1. The statement was taken from an article in the *Washington Post* that reported on a recent conference, cosponsored by the Sante Fe Institute and the Los Alamos National Laboratory, entitled "The Artificial Life II Conference." The conference was dedicated to exploring how billions of years of biological evolution can be used as the basis for developing design strategies for new computer technologies. Farmer, who organized the conference, made the following statement about the long-term prospects of the research program in which the participants at the conference were engaged:

> With the advent of artificial life, we may be the first species to create its own successors. What will these successors be like? If we fail in our task as creators, they may indeed be cold and malevolent. However, if we succeed, they may be glorious enlightened creatures that far surpass us in their intelligence and wisdom. It is is quite possible that, when the conscious beings of the future look back on this era, we

will be most noteworthy not in and of ourselves but
for what we gave rise to. Artificial life is potentially
the most beautiful creation of humanity. To shun artificial life without deeper consideration reflects a
shallow anthropomorphism.[19]

My response to this statement is that it is "shallow
anthropomorphism" that lies at the heart of such technological megalomania, and that a deeper or more profound
understanding of our anthropomorphism would have the
very opposite effect. It would lead to the recognition that
the "most beautiful creation of humanity" would be a
world in which the needs of all human beings are more
effectively and amply met and served. It is also worth
noting that the most famous of the megalomanic dreams
to be realized at Los Alamos was the birth of another
technology that could serve to eliminate the human gene
pool: the atomic bomb. And there is another large irony
here. A world inhabited by our "descendants" in the form
of AI systems capable of self-replication—however superior they might be in the scope and range of their cognitive
abilities—and a world reduced to radioactive dust and ash
by global thermonuclear war would be quite similar in two
important respects. Both would be barren of conscious
beings and both would come into existence due to our
failure to understand the insidious role that reification
plays in the construction of human reality. Reification in
both of these instances would be extended to its ultimate
conclusion, in that human beings would have created realities that deny themselves in a quite literal sense. If consciousness is to evolve on this planet in the service of the
ultimate value, we must, I think, quickly come to the realization that reality for human beings is a human product
with a human history, and thereby dispel the tendency to
view any "product" of our world-constructing minds as
anything more, or other, than a human artifact.

Yet if the two cultures are to join hands in the vital
business of properly evaluating the use-value of new AI

computer technologies in the service of the ultimate value, it seems clear that arguments based on the first-person perspective of practical reason will not provide the now missing foundations for common understanding and meaningful dialogue. The arguments advanced by humanists–social scientists based on this perspective appeal, as we have seen, to some version of Cartesian dualism, and thus posit the existence of a domain of reality that cannot be reduced to or described in terms of physical law and theory. Yet this dualism will not and cannot be taken seriously by those who are thoroughly inducted into the culture of scientists-engineers. The challenge is to demonstrate from the third-person perspective of theoretical reason that human consciousness on the physical substrate of the human brain is more primary and important than consciousness on any other physical substrate.

If we could provide such a demonstration, it could serve to remove the principal stumbling block that now stands in the way of meaningful dialogue between the two cultures. The area of scientific knowledge that appears to have provided fundamental insights into the life of the cosmos, and that allows us to argue for a fundamental distinction between consciousness as an emergent property of the human brain and any alternate form of consciousness that we can create on another physical substrate, is modern theoretical physics. Understanding the implications of modern physical theories as they will be considered in the next chapter requires no background in higher mathematics or physics. What is required, however, is a willingness to free oneself from what William Blake termed the "mind-forged manacles" of our everyday sense of reality.

CHAPTER 8

Paradigms, Paradoxes, and the Technological Future

*The shift in emphasis from things to functions
is what distinguishes the old physics from the
new physics. In the neurosciences, what's
needed is a similar shift in attention from brain
centers and pathways toward brain processes
and functions. We must view the brain as a
dynamic process that partakes of the mystery
and wonder of all matter in the universe. The
new physics will help us do that.*
                                    —Richard Restak, M.D.
                                    The Brain

In order to fully appreciate how persuasive the more sophisticated scientific legitimation of the AI evolution-of-
consciousness hypothesis can appear from the third-person perspective of theoretical reason, a brief review of how
its advocates view the evolution of the universe is helpful.
In this view, the universe is a vast information-processing
system that is evolving toward increasingly more complex
levels of organization. Assuming that this evolutionary
tendency did not exhaust itself on Earth with the appearance of the human brain, the advocates predict that the

information-processing capabilities of this brain will soon be eclipsed by the information-processing capabilities of AI computer systems built on inorganic substrates. In the next stage of this natural and inevitable evolutionary process, according to some advocates of the hypothesis, we will witness the birth of a conscious AI computer on a biological substrate. Since an AI computer operating on the molecular or organic level could, in theory at least, store, process, and manipulate vast amounts of information per unit of time, its conscious awareness of self and world should be considerably more extended and refined than we can now imagine. This explains why some advocates of the hypothesis welcome the prospect that AI computer systems on biological substrates and capable of self-replication will be our conscious descendants. The prospect that such a computer could exist makes it possible to circumvent our previous objection that natural selection does not operate on inorganic matter and cannot, therefore, be assumed to legislate over the evolution of conscious AI systems. Since there is every reason to suppose that natural selection would operate on AI computer systems residing in biological substrates, the contention that consciousness in these systems is unnatural or artificial would seem to have no basis in scientific fact. If we eventually come to view the universe—as many experts in systems theory, modern biology, and physics contend that we will—as nothing more or less than a vast information-processing system, the emergence of consciousness in AI systems that are also self-replicating biological organisms could simply mean that information processing in our corner of the universe has evolved to a higher level of complexity.

My own attempt to refute the more sophisticated scientific legitimation of the AI evolution-of-consciousness hypothesis from the third-person perspective of theoretical reason appeals to modern theoretical physics. It is my conviction that this physics forces us to conclude that the emergence of consciousness on the physical substrate of the human brain is intimately connected with the evolution of the entire cosmos, from its origins to the present, in ways that cannot in principle apply to the emergence of consciousness on any other physical substrates. Equally important, I also hope to demonstrate that the world view of modern theoretical physics serves to dispel the notion that we are merely cogs in a giant machine or, to use terminology that is now closer to home, merely micro- or minicomputers in the giant supercomputer of the universe.

Although some advocates of the AI evolution-of-consciousness hypothesis are physicists with considerable expertise in modern theoretical physics, they appear to have systematically ignored the challenges that modern theoretical physics pose to the classical understanding of the relationship between mind and matter. Theoretical physicists in increasing numbers have come to view the mind-matter problem in terms that are quite different from the view required by the hardcore materialism that characterized nineteenth-century physics. This does not mean that these physicists have chosen to deal with the mind-matter problem outside of the framework of theoretical reason, or that they have resorted to arguments that appeal to Cartesian dualism. Rather, they have chosen to reconsider the relationship between mind and matter for the simple reason that the description of the character of physical reality in modern physical theories has made the view of that relationship problematic. Although it will not be possible in one chapter to review every aspect of the complex debate among theoretical physicists concerning the mind-matter problem, I do hope to demonstrate that *all* scientific legitimations of the AI evolution-of-consciousness hypothesis are based on outmoded scientific assumptions about the character of the life of the universe.

The First Scientific Revolution

Unrestricted determinism, which the advocates of the AI evolution-of-consciousness hypothesis appear to endorse, became a basic construct in Western thought with the advent of classical physics. The success of this physics was due largely to the extension and refinement of a language system that is quite different from ordinary written or spoken language: the language of mathematical and geometrical forms. The description of physical reality that emerged in the seventeenth and eighteenth centuries was based upon the newly invented branches of mathematics known as calculus and analytical geometry. Yet the architects of the first scientific revolution—Copernicus, Galileo, Descartes, Kepler, and Newton—were spared the metaphysical angst associated with the clockwork universe, largely because of how they understood the character of mathematical and geometrical forms. All of these figures conceived of the language of mathematical physics as the primary means through which mortal man could commune with the forms resident in the eternal mind of God, and from their pespective doing physics was an act of communion with the divine. Yet even in the eighteenth century, any overt appeal to the metaphysical in the actual conduct of physics became unfashionable. Physics, or the science of mechanics, was increasingly regarded, as the philosopher of science Ivor Leclerc puts it, as "an autonomous science," and any alleged role of God was viewed as "deus ex machina."[1]

The contemporary view of the character of scientific knowledge, or at least the view that is most widely endorsed from the third-person perspective of theoretical reason, is positivism. This doctrine, formulated in the nineteenth century by figures like Ernst Mach, Heinrich Hertz, and Jules-Henri Poincaré, states that "true, genuine, and certain knowledge" is revealed in the mathematical description, and that all metaphysical concerns are, by definition, excluded. The triumph of the doctrine of positivism also explains in large part the inability of scientists-engineers to take seriously arguments against the AI evolution-of-consciousness hypothesis advanced by humanists–social scientists.

Since these arguments are premised on extrascientific or

metaphysical assumptions that are not amenable to mathematical description and that cannot, therefore, be disclosed in terms of "true, genuine, and certain knowledge," those thoroughly inducted into the culture of scientists-engineers cannot help but view them as arbitrary and capricious. When we also remind ourselves that mathematical physics, or the hard sciences generally, have been undermining the truths of practical reason with remarkable consistency for three hundred years, the positions taken by the humanists-social scientists seem weaker still. The damage done by the triumph of the scientific in these terms, according to historian of science Alexander Koyré, is as follows:

> Yet there is something for which Newton—or better to say not Newton alone, but modern science in general—can still be made responsible: it is the splitting of our world in two. I have been saying that modern science broke down the barriers that separated the heavens from the earth and that it united and unified the universe. And that is true. But, as I have said too, it did this by substituting the world of quality and sense perception for another world—the world of quantity, or reified geometry, a world in which, though there is a place for everything, there is no place for man. Thus the world of science—the real world—became estranged and utterly divorced from the world of life, which science has been unable to explain—not even to explain away by calling it "subjective." True, these worlds are everyday—and even more and more—connected by praxis. Yet they are divided by an abyss. Two worlds: this means two truths. Or no truth at all. This is the tragedy of the modern mind which "solved the riddle of the universe," but only to replace it by another riddle: the riddle of itself.[2]

As neuroscience begins to map the terra incognita of "subjective" reality in terms of the true, genuine, and certain knowledge of mathematical science, this tragic sense of estrangement between the "real world" and the "world of life" could become far more acute. If all of the mysteries we associate with mind are eventually mapped in scientific detail, in the absence of any profound revisions in our normative understanding of natural process and the truths of science, our existential anxiety could increase enormously.

Yet the abyss between mind and world described by Koyré is principally due to the fact that classical physics made no provisions for the knowing mind. In classical physics, nature was viewed as forces acting between mass points in the abstract background of space and time. The universe was represented as a vast machine in which collections of mass points interacted with one another in terms of external forces. In this model the knowing self was necessarily separate, discrete, atomized, and achieved its knowledge of physical reality from the "outside" of physical systems. As the theoretical physicist Henry Stapp puts it, "Classical physics not only fails to demand the mental, it fails to even provide a rational place for the mental. And if the mental is introduced ad hoc, then it must remain totally ineffectual, in absolute contradiction to our deepest experience."[3] In modern physics, as I now hope to demonstrate, the status of the knowing mind is utterly different.

The Brave New World of Modern Physics

The most startling feature of modern theoretical physics, a feature that has become increasingly apparent since Einstein's special theory of relativity (1905), is that "wholeness" seems implicit in all physical processes. For those accustomed to associating the term *wholeness* with Eastern metaphysical thought, let me emphasize that from the third-person perspective of theoretical reason, the term has nothing to do with metaphysics. It refers to an actual property of physical reality that manifests in both theory and experiment on the most fundamental level, and that exists in complementary relation to all emergent or measurable physical phenomena. In other words, the separability or the distinctness of matter now appears to be an emergent aspect of an underlying unity.

The special theory of relativity challenged separability with the view of matter as an infinitely mutable expression of conserved energy in accordance with the relation $E = mc^2$, and with the view of space and time as seamlessly connected in a continuum. Separability was challenged once again in the general theory of relativity (1915), which requires that we view fundamental constants, physical laws, and primary entities as intimately linked in a unified field of space-time curvature. All measurements in relativity theory are dependent upon the relative velocity of the reference frame within which the measurement is made. Since every frame is related to every other frame, like the rotation of axes in a four-dimensional continuum, it is the mutual relation of entities that determines their nature and properties.

Another challenge to separability posed by the general theory involves an entirely new understanding of the relationship between matter and field. The effect of gravity, concluded Einstein, is to curve the space-time continuum. The terrain of space-time can be crudely visualized as mountainous in the region of large or massive bodies, like our sun, and as a flat plane in regions of space where there is very little matter. "We may therefore regard matter," wrote Einstein, "as being constituted by the regions in space in which the fields are extremely intense[4] (see Figure 15).

The relation between part and whole represented in relativity theory was immediately understood as utterly new and profound by those capable of comprehending the mathematical description. According to Einstein's field theory, wrote Max Planck, "each individual particle of the system in a certain sense, at any one time, exists simultaneously in every part of the space occupied by the system."[5] And the system, Planck takes care to explain, is the entire universe. As Einstein put it, "Physical reality must be described in terms of continuous functions in space. The material point, therefore, can hardly be conceived any more as the basic concept of the theory."[6] With the elimination of the classical notion of discreteness, the collection of matter that constitutes the idealization of "self" as separate from the whole becomes, suggests Einstein, merely an illusion:

> A human being is a part of the whole, called by us the "Universe," a part limited in time and space. He experiences himself, his thoughts and feelings as something separate from the rest—a kind of optical illusion of consciousness. This delusion is a kind of prison for us, restricting us to our personal desires and to affection for a few persons nearest to us. Our task must be to free ourselves from the prison by widening our circle of compassion to embrace all living creatures and the whole of nature in its beauty. Nobody is able to achieve this completely, but the striving for such achievement is in itself a part of the liberation and a foundation for inner security.[7]

Figure 15

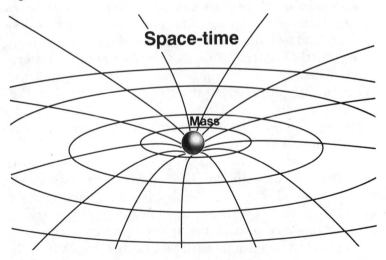

Warped space-time around a gravitating mass.

The theme of nonseparability or wholeness was considerably amplified with the advent of quantum mechanics in the 1920s and 1930s. Although quantum mechanics first challenged the notion of separability in the relationship between observer and observed system, it has also consistently led to larger unifications between part and whole. As Henry Stapp describes this progress, "Quantum theory unified position and momentum. And the recent development of gauge theories, supersymmetries, and string theories exhibit again and again always the overcoming of prejudice of the separateness of things, and the creation of mathematical structures in which formerly separate elements become parts of a more cohesive unity."[8]

Quantum Field Theory

The concepts of fields and their associated quanta are now fundamental to our understanding of the character of physical reality. The essential paradox confronted in quantum field theory is wave-particle dualism, which can be crudely illustrated as follows: view the particle as a point-like something, like the period at the end of this sentence, and the wave as continuous and spread out. Quantum physics has demonstrated in both theory and experiment that all quanta exhibit both of these complementary aspects. Yet the obvious logical problem is, how can a point-like something localized in space and time, the particle, also be the spread out and continuous something, the wave (see Figure 16)?

In order to illustrate that quanta, or matter as it manifests on the most fundamental level, exhibit both of these aspects, let us briefly discuss the famous two-hole experiment. As physicist Richard Feynmann puts it, "Any situation in quantum mechanics, as it turns out, can always be explained by saying, 'You remember the case with the experiment with the two holes? It's the same thing.'"[9] Consider an idealized two-hole experiment. We have a source of quanta, in this case electrons, an electron gun

Figure 16   Wave and Particle

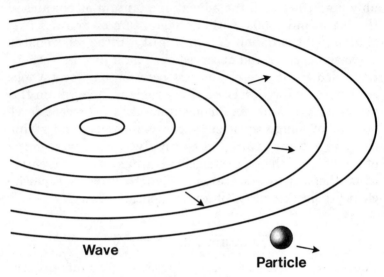

A wave is not localized, whereas a particle is localized.

like that in your television set, and a screen with two openings that are small enough to be comparable to the wavelength of the electron. The openings can be narrow slits, as in Thomas Young's famous experiments, or round holes—the only requirement is that the holes or slits be small enough to be comparable to the wavelength of the electron. The detector is a second screen, like a television screen, that flashes when an electron impacts (see Figure 17).

Since the wave aspect of the electron will reveal itself in our experiment with the presence of interference patterns, it is important to understand this basic feature of all wave phenomena. Interference patterns result when two waves, interacting with one another, produce peaks in places where they combine and troughs where they cancel one another out. Anyone who has spent some time watching ocean waves move toward a beach is familiar with this aspect of wave phenomena. If two equally large waves come together, or two waves whose heights or amplitudes are similar, they will combine to produce a much larger wave. Similarly, if the trough of one wave is the same as the height of another as they combine, the two waves will cancel one another out. In our experiment, interference patterns appear when both slits, S_2 and S_3, are open and produce bands of light and dark on the screen. The bands of light and dark indicate the presence of interference patterns and demonstrate that the wave aspect of the electron is being recorded. If, however, we close one of the two slits, the result will be a bright spot on the screen indicating that the electrons have impacted the screen in direct line with the electron gun. Since we see no interference patterns, this result indicates that the electrons moved

Figure 17 Two-Hole Experiment

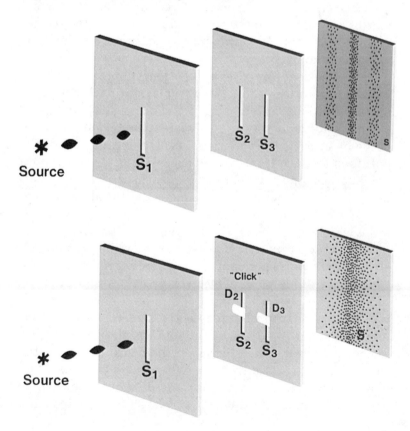

through the one slit as particles, like unimaginably small bullets. If we view the quantum reality as consisting of either wave or particle, it is as if the electrons somehow "know" whether or not both slits are open and behave accordingly.

Recently physicists have been able to conduct a two-slit experiment with a single particle and its associated wave packet. Viewing the single electron as particle, or as a point-like something, with both slits open we would expect it to travel through one slit or the other—how could a particle localized in space and time travel through both slits simultaneously? Yet if we conduct this experiment many times with a single particle with both slits open, interference patterns associated with the wave aspect of the electron will appear on our detector screen. It does not matter how much elapsed time there is between the release of the single particles or whether we make the elapsed time variable or even completely random—we will still witness interference patterns after a sufficient number of individual electrons travel through our apparatus with both slits open. Even more interesting, we could conduct identical experiments in a thousand different laboratories using only one particle in each experiment, superimpose all the points of impact from the thousand detector screens on one another, and we would still witness interference patterns associated with the wave aspect of the electron.

Let us refine our experiment a bit in an effort to determine which of the slits the electron in its particle aspect passes through by putting detectors (D_2 and D_3) at each slit (S_2 and S_3). We accomplish this by covering each of the two slits with an array of electron detectors that allow us to detect the presence of an electron as it moves through the apparatus toward the detector screen. Assume that many electrons have passed through the slits, and that we know from our detectors which of the two slits each of the electrons has traveled through. What would be revealed on our detector screen in this case would be two bright spots in direct line with the slit that our detector indicated each electron passed through. Our attempt to measure or observe what happens at each slit with detectors has resulted in a situation in which only the particle aspect of the total reality is revealed.

If we once again view the electron as either a wave or a particle, the results in this experiment appear even more bizarre than in our previous experiment—the electrons behave as if they not only "know" whether the two slits are open but also whether we are watching or recording them with our instruments. Yet the orthodox scientific view of this situation says that our commonsense understanding of matter, or of any material substance, as well as our tendency to relie on either-or logic, simply does not apply here. For reasons we will explore shortly, the wave-particle aspects of quantum reality are emergent phenomena in a universe in which parts are manifestations of an undivided whole.

For the non-physicist it is not immediately apparent what the curious results of the two-hole or two-slit experiments have to do with the physical world in which we take our being. The answer is that what is disclosed in these experiments are general properties of all quanta, and thus fundamental aspects of everything in physical reality. Material reality as described in quantum field theory is constituted by the transformation and organization of fields and their associated quanta. The exchange of quanta in and between fields accounts for the emergence and evolution of all events in the vast cosmos from its origins to the present. Interactions between the four known fields—gravity, electromagnetism, the weak, and the strong—are mediated by the exchange of the following quanta: the graviton for gravity, the photon for electromagnetism, the intermediate bosons for the weak force, and the colored gluons for the strong or nuclear force (see Figure 18). In terms of quantum field theory, all that has ever existed or will ever exist in the vast cosmos reduces to interactions between quanta and fields.

The particle-wave dualism that constitutes complemen-

Figure 18 Four Fundamental Interactions: Strong, Electromagnetic, Weak, and Gravitational

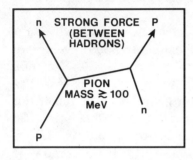

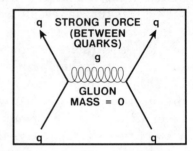

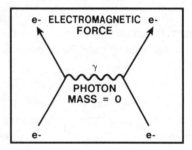

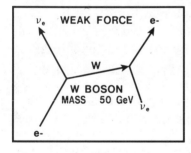

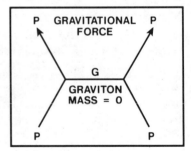

tary aspects of all quanta, and that explains the results of the two-slit experiments, can be understood in part by realizing that any change or transition in the state of quanta occurs in terms of specific chunks of energy. Nature is quite adamant about this, and there are no in-between amounts of energy involved. Less than the specific chunk of energy means no quantum transitions, and it is only whole chunks of energy that are present in transitions. This chunk of energy is known as Plank's constant and is represented by a specific amount of action equal to 6.6 × 10⁻²⁷ erg second. If Planck's constant were zero, a particle would have no wave properties and a wave no particle properties. Since Planck's constant is not zero, the mathematical description indicates that the spread, or uncertainty, of momentum is greater than, or possibly equal to, the value of the constant, or, more accurately, Planck's constant divided by 2π. This relationship was first formalized by Werner Heisenberg in his famous indeterminacy principle. The principle states that the product of the uncertainty in measuring momentum, p, of a quantum particle times the uncertainty in measuring its position, x, is always equal to or greater than Planck's constant. In the language of mathematics, the principle is written as $\Delta x \, \Delta p \geq \hbar$, where the symbol Δx denotes the uncertainty of measuring position, x, and Δp denotes the uncertainty of measuring momentum, p (see Figure 19).

Figure 19   Wave Packet

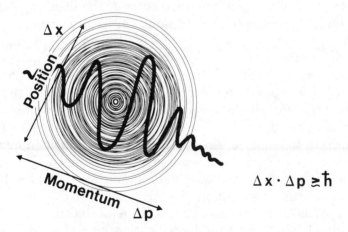

$$\Delta x \cdot \Delta p \geq \hbar$$

Illustration of Heisenberg's indeterminacy principle: (uncertainty in position) times (certainty in momentum) is at least as large as Planck's constant divided by 2π.

In quantum physics the total reality of a quantum system, like the electron in our two-slit experiment, is described in terms of two disparate theories for each aspect: wave mechanics and matrix mechanics. Wave mechanics is completely deterministic and describes the continuous movement in time of a multidimensional spread-out wave. Wave mechanics describes everything that can be known about the quantum system with one mind-boggling qualification: it can do so only in the absence of observation. What makes this situation strange is that we are accustomed in everyday experience to conceiving of ourselves and external objects as utterly separate and discrete. The view of the actual character of physical reality in quantum physics suggests, however, that this is a macro-level illusion. From the perspective of quantum physics, all seemingly separate and discrete collections of matter, including ourselves, are inextricably interconnected. How this condition explains why all the possibilities given in the wave equation cannot be observed or realized in any single act of observation will concern us in a moment.

Matrix mechanics, in contrast with wave mechanics, deals only in measurable quantities or observables. A matrix is essentially a generalization of the idea of simple number to a square or rectangular array of numbers, and the result when two matrices are multiplied depends on the order of the multiplication. When we normally multiply numbers, the order in which they are multiplied is irrelevant. A × B or B × A yield the same reliable results. In the quantum domain, however, the presence of indeterminacy means that the order of multiplication does make a difference. In the language of mathematics, variables in quantum physics do not commute, and matrix mechanics is a useful way of dealing with noncommuting variables, like position and momentum.

Put another way, we have in wave mechanics a mathematical formalism that describes quantum phenomena in terms of a multidimensional wave with well-defined characteristics. Yet when we observe what would otherwise appear to be mathematically real or actual properties of the wave function by making measurements or observations, some of the possibilities appear while others do not. Although the range of possibilities can be derived in terms of the wave function, or by squaring its amplitude, $|\Psi|^2$, when an actual measurement or observation is made, the various possibilities become one actuality. What this means is that what is finally observed can be predicted only within the constraints of quantum indeterminacy. In other words, we are obliged to deal here only in probabilities that certain results will occur; we cannot in principle predict results with the utmost certainty (see Figure 20).

Figure 20   Probability in Wave Function

A. Prior to Measurement

B. After Measurement

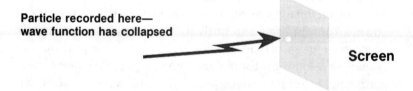

The square of the wave function gives the probability of finding the particle somewhere prior to the act of measurement. After the measurement, the wave function is said to collapse, and the particle is found at a specific location in space.

The orthodox interpretation of this situation, formulated principally by Danish physicist Niels Bohr, obliges us to view wave and particle aspects of quantum reality, along with their associated mathematical formalism, in terms of the principle of complementarity. According to Bohr, the principle must be invoked in quantum physics for the following reasons: (1) wave and particle aspects of quantum processes constitute a complete description of the total reality; and (2) each aspect of this reality displaces the other in any single act of observation. Therefore, the best we can do in our efforts to coordinate our experience with the quantum domain from the third-person perspective of theoretical reason is, says Bohr, to attempt to keep both complementary aspects of the total reality in mind as we deal with this reality.

The complementary constructs at work in making observations or measurements of a quantum system are interaction and noninteraction with the system. Each precludes the other in any single act of observation, and yet both are required to properly analyze or understand the experimental results. The reason why this must in principle be the case in a quantum mechanical universe is that the experimenter and the experimental apparatus, or the observer and the observed system, cannot be viewed as separate and discrete. Both are manifestations of one unified quantum system, and experimental results can be realistically evaluated only if we view them as emergent phenomena of this system.

According to the Copenhagen Interpretation, when we make observations or measurements we are not forcing a quanta to "choose" one path in the array of mathematically real possibilities given by the wave equation, or "causing" some mathematically real possibilities to appear and others to disappear. We can assume that we disturb or create phenomena via observation or measurement only if we make the prior assumption that the quantum system can be described independently of observation or measurement. Since that condition clearly does not per-

tain, the only way in which we can realistically comprehend the emergent phenomena represented by the experimental results is by factoring in the presence of the
observer and his or her observational choices. There is, in
short, no godlike perspective from which we can know this
reality. It can be known only within the framework of a
mathematical formalism featuring quantum indeterminacy and wave-particle dualism. And our analysis of
those arrangements and results must be premised on the
assumption that the observer and the observed phenomena
are inseparably interconnected.

We should note in passing that the orthodox Copenhagen Interpretation has probably occasioned more discord
in the community of physicists than any other orthodox
interpretation in the history of science. Although the various positions taken in the debate over the efficacy of this
interpretation are much too detailed and complex to discuss here, we should at least note some of the principal
sources of disagreement. If one assumes, as Bohr did and
as all the recent progress in mathematical physics attests,
that we live in a quantum mechanical universe, we confront here the prospect that the magnificent exactitude of
physics has been reduced to dealing in probabilities. And
we also confront in the Copenhagen Interpretation a direct and frontal assault on the doctrine of positivism.

If our mathematical description of nature obliges us to
deal in probabilities, as opposed to exact and totally predictable actualities, what does this imply about the notion
that "true, genuine, and certain" knowledge is revealed in
the mathematical description? Although Bohr never wa-
vered in his conviction that mathematical physics was the
language system that allows us to coordinate our experience with nature in the most precise and complete terms
possible, he was, nevertheless, driven to the conclusion
that the doctrine of positivism was outmoded. The more
realistic view, claimed Bohr, is that mathematical physics
is a language system whose real or actual existence is in
our subjective reality, and that the "truth" value of any

propositions expressed in this language is utterly dependent upon whether predictions are borne out in repeatable
scientific experiments under controlled conditions.[10]

Although the community of physicists continues to
struggle with the implications of wave-particle dualism,
there is concensus regarding one major implication of
modern physical theories: the universe is an unbroken and
undissectable dynamic whole. From the perspective of
modern physics, the classical view of the atom as a discrete and immutable building block in material reality
makes no sense at all. An atom as we now view it, notes
Henry Stapp, "turns out to be nothing but the potentiali-
ties in the behavior pattern of others. What we find, therefore, are not elementary space-time realities, but rather a
web of relationships in which no part can stand alone;
every part derives its meaning and existence from its
place within the whole."[11] What this means, as Stephen
Jay Gould suggested earlier, is that a purely reductionist
approach to understanding physical reality is no longer
viable. In this new situation, the complete description of
any particular phenomenon would require that we comprehend the entire web of relation between this phenomenon
and the universe as a whole. Also, from this new perspective matter cannot be dissected from the omnipresent sea
of energy that is the other aspect of its being, nor can we
in theory or in fact observe matter from the outside.

Bell's Theorem and the Aspect Experiments

Nonseparability, or wholeness, as a fundamental feature
of the life of the cosmos has been massively reinforced of
late by the results of experiments conducted by Alain Aspect and his team at the University of Paris-South, published in 1982.[12] These experiments were the last in a
series of experiments designed to test some predictions
made in a mathematical theorem published by John Bell
of the Centre for European Nuclear Research in 1964.[13]

One of the primary tenents of classical physics is the
assumption of locality, meaning that we should not be able

to witness correlations in experiments at observational points that are "space-like separated" from one another. In other words, if the regions in space from which we attempt to make observations of potentially correlatable phenomena are sufficiently distant from one another so that a signal traveling at light speed could not carry information between them in the time allowed for observation, these regions are understood to be space-like separated. The assumption until recently was that it would be quite impossible to observe correlations between events in space-like separated regions because light speed, in accordance with relativity theory, is the upper limit at which signals can travel in the universe. Since relativity theory has not been violated and light speed remains the upper limit at which signals can propagate between two points, this fact of nature has also served as the foundation for what is known as the assumption of locality.

The assumption of locality means that if we are conducting experiments on any phenomenon in nature that can be assumed to be sufficiently distant from any other potentially correlatable phenomenon as to disallow the prospect that signals traveling at light speed can explain the results, we can safely assume that the phenomenon being studied is effectively isolated or separated from the rest of the cosmos. What Bell showed mathematically is that the formalism of quantum physics does allow for correlations between results in space-like separated regions and, therefore, violates the assumption of locality. The mathematical statement derived in Bell's theorem is known as Bell's inequality. Physical theories based on the assumption of locality, known as local realistic theories, would obey this inequality, whereas physical theories like quantum theory would violate it. Since Bell's theorem demonstrated mathematically that either locality or nonlocality was a fact of nature, the challenge became to devise experiments that could unambiguously determine which of these alleged facts of nature was valid.

When Bell published his theorem, neither he nor anyone else knew what the answer would be. The only way to answer the question raised in the theorem was to appeal to the court of last resort in physical science: repeatable scientific experiments under controlled conditions. What finally settled the question was the publication of the results of Alain Aspect's experiments. These experiments were based on the experimentally verified assumption in quantum physics that quanta having a common origin in a unified quantum system—like the annihilation of a positron-electron pair, the return of an electron to its ground state, or the separation of a pair of photons from the singlet state—will display properties that correlate with one another in terms of their shared wave function.

The quanta used in the Aspect experiments were quanta of light, or photons. The experiments were designed to study the properties of a two-photon system that correlate with one another when the photons originate from a singlet state. The correlatable properties studied were angles of polarization of the two-photon system, as each photon traveled in opposite directions from the other on a well-defined axis after originating at one source in a singlet state. Polarization defines a direction in space associated with the wave aspect of the photon. Although polarization in introductory physics textbooks is normally explained in terms of horizontal and vertical polarization, a fact of nature exploited by manufacturers of sunglasses, the variety of polarization studied in the Aspect experiments is known as circular polarization. This form of polarization can be crudely visualized as a twirling baton with a particular orientation in its motion that is characterized as either left-handed or right-handed, in terms of orientation along the shared axis. What quantum theory predicts in this experimental situation is that if we conduct a sufficient number of experiments on this two-photon system, we will witness a rather exact correlation in terms of various angles of polarization of the two photons along the common axis.

Since prior experiments designed to test the predictions of Bell's theorem had already confirmed correlations in such two-photon systems in space-like separated regions, the Aspect experiments were designed to prove or disprove an explanation for these correlations that allowed one to suppose that locality had not been violated. The explanation was that the wave function at the source of the two-photon system carried information between the two space-like separated regions. Although the notion that a single wave function could carry information over any distance from one source instantaneously as if it were one unified wave function seemed a bit odd, it was at least a basis for denying the existence of nonlocality. To test the validity of this explanation, an experimental arrangement was needed in which the state of the two-photon system could be altered when the photons were in flight from their source in the singlet state.

Aspect and his team accomplished this by allowing optical switches to choose between the orientations of the polarization analyzers while the photons were in flight from the singlet state (see Figure 21). The beam was directed toward either one of the two polarizing filters, which measure a direction in polarization, and each filter had its own photon detector behind it. The switching of the two orientations required only two nanoseconds, or 10×10^{-9} seconds, and was triggered by an automated device that generated a pseudorandom signal. Since the distance between the two filters was thirteen meters, no signal traveling at light speed could be presumed to carry information between the two filters, as a light signal would require forty nanoseconds to travel from one filter to another. What this means, assuming that no signal can travel faster than light, is that the choice of the orientation measured on the right filter should not influence the transmission of information in the photon that travels through the left filter. And yet the opposite proved to be the case. The correlations observed in the polarizations of this two-photon system were precisely as quantum physics predicted they would be.

In order to appreciate how strange these results are, even from the third-person perspective of theoretical reason, we must first remind ourselves that relativity theory

Figure 21   The Aspect Experiment

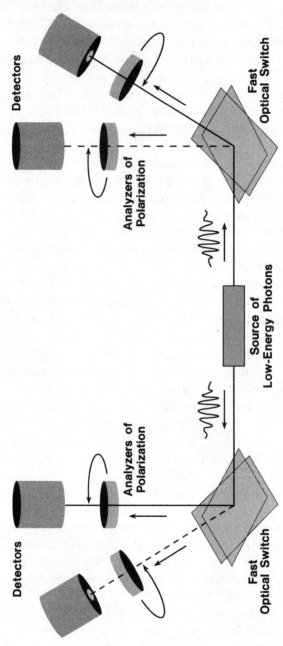

The experimental setup carried out by Aspect and his coworkers to test the predictions of quantum theory versus the predictions of local realistic theories. Thus there is now general agreement that the experiments testing Bell's theorem have made local realistic theories, like deterministic hidden variables, scientifically gratuitous at best.

has not been violated, and thus we must still presume that no signal can travel between space-like separated regions at speeds faster than light. Also, there is no reason in principle why the results of these experiments would not be precisely the same regardless of the distance between the space-like separated detectors. If, for example, the source of the two-photon system were halfway to the edge of the known universe, detector A was on earth, and detector B was on the edge of the known universe, the results, assuming that points A and B were equidistant from the source, should be the same as those recorded in the laboratory. Also, all indications are that the correlations in the actual experiments occur in "no time," or that they are truly instantaneous. In other words, the observed correlations appear to be occurring beyond space-time at a level of physical reality at which nonseparability or wholeness is a fact of nature.

More important, nonlocality cannot be assumed to be a fact of nature only in the special laboratory conditions in the experiments testing Bell's theorem. As physicist Bernard d'Espagnet has pointed out, nonlocality must be viewed as a universal or cosmic phenomenon.[14] In the history of the cosmos, all quanta can safely be presumed to have interacted with other quanta in a unified quantum system, and thus all quanta can be viewed as a single quantum system. Some atoms in our bodies interacted in a single quantum state in close proximity to the cosmic fireball at the origins of the cosmos, and other quanta that interacted in that state are located in the most distant star. This means, however strange it might seem, that the quanta that make up our bodies are as much a part of a unified system as the photons propagating in opposite directions in the Aspect experiments. Thus nonlocality or nonseparability in these experiments translates into the vastly grander notion of nonlocality or nonseparability as a factual condition in the entire universe. For those who are inclined to view this new fact of nature as a basis for a faster-than-light communications technology, this is simply not the case. The correlations studied in the Aspect

**Figure 22   Evolution of the Universe: The Big Bang
Theory**

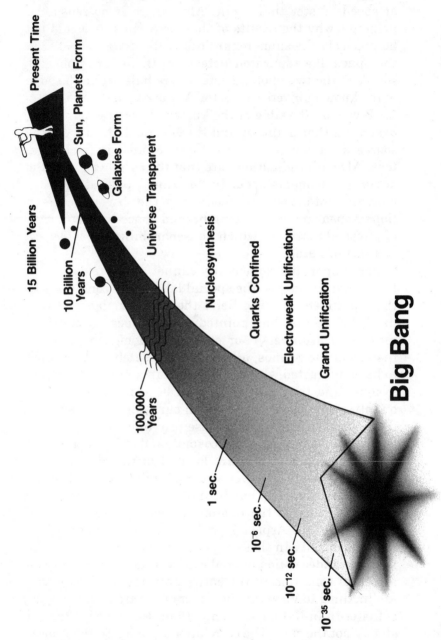

and other similar experiments exist in quanta that originate in a unified quantum system in accordance with quantum indeterminacy. What this means is that any information that originates at the source is random and cannot, therefore, carry information. The pattern in one photon of the two-photon system makes nonrandom sense only if we are able to compare it with the pattern observed in the other photon. Any information contained in the entire system can be derived only from observations of both paired photons, or from comparisons of the differences between the two random patterns. This also means that nonlocality as a fact of nature provides no support whatsoever for unrestricted determinism or, more accurately, that it argues against the existence of unrestricted determinism.

Mind, Brain, and Modern Physical Theory

Philosopher of science Errol Harris has drawn upon the new understanding of the relationship between part and whole in modern physical theory to make a rather convincing case—however strange the notion might initially appear—that the entire universe is conscious. He begins with the assumption that our most advanced scientific knowledge suggests that the human brain is part of a progressive order in the evolution of the cosmos, in which each phase is a summation and transformation of all previous phases. From this perspective the history of the evolution of consciousness does not begin even with the first ancestor of DNA, which appears in the fossil records some 4.5 billion years ago. It begins at the beginning, or with the origins of the cosmos in the Big Bang. And all the intervening developments are intimately connected with our present existence as conscious beings (see Figure 22).

The central feature of Harris's argument is the new understanding of the character of wholeness or nonseparability in the life of the cosmos, an understanding that has been consistently reinforced by every major advance in modern physical theory and that was dramatically confirmed in the experiments testing Bell's theorem. Harris begins by pointing out that a unity without internal content is a blank or empty set and is not recognizable as a whole. A collection of merely externally related parts does not constitute a genuine whole, he argues, because the parts in such a whole must be "mutually adaptive and complementary to one another."[15]

Harris distinguishes between genuine wholes and spurious wholes. In a genuine whole, the relationships between the constituent parts must be internal or immanent in the parts. In a spurious whole, the parts appear to disclose wholeness due to relationships that are external to the parts.[16] The collection of parts that allegedly constitute the whole in classical physics is an example of such a spurious whole. According to Harris, parts constitute a genuine whole when what he terms the universal ordering principle is "inside" the parts and thereby adjusts each to all so that they interlock and become mutually complementary. The terms and relations between parts in such a whole will have in common the imminent principle of order, which is the "structure of the system to which they belong."[17] Since this description of wholeness is consistent with both relativity theory and quantum physics, Harris argues that each stage of progressive order in the cosmos "sublates" that which has gone before. In other words, progressive order is a process in which each phase is a summation and transformation of the previous phase, incorporating the entire series of phases or transformations through which it has developed and as a result of which it assumes its own structure.

Harris then suggests that if consciousness manifests or emerges in the later stages of the life of the universe, then it would follow that the universe has always been, in some sense, conscious. Consciousness as a property of the entire cosmos is not, however, understood here in any anthropomorphic sense, or in terms of any constructs that have emerged in the symbolic universe of members of any culture. Consciousness is defined rather as self-reflective awareness of itself as "reality-in-itself," an awareness that manifests in the order that is required to create a universe that is "something" when it could just as well have been "nothing." Since consciousness for human beings can be defined on the most basic level as the ability of the neuronal organization of our brains to generate self-reflective awareness founded upon a sense of internal consistency or order, then the universe in these terms can also be assumed, concludes Harris, to be conscious.

If we can accept this argument, then consciousness as an emergent property of the physical substrate of the human brain is not only intimately connected to the entire history of the cosmos; it also partakes of the consciousness of the universe itself. It is important to emphasize here that in the absence of unrestricted determinism, we cannot ascribe any "intentionality" in the life of the cosmos that would allow us to conclude that the emergence of consciousness in ourselves was in any sense preordained or inevitable. Yet we are provided here with a view of human consciousness as inextricably interconnected with all prior events in the cosmos, and with an understanding of this consciousness that assumes that it displays "tendencies to recur" which appear endemic in the self-organizing dynamics of the entire universe from its origins to the present. If we also assume, as all the evidence from the social sciences suggests, that the content of human consciousness, or our linguistic and cultural programming, was a "free" creation of human beings, then any form of consciousness that we elect to create is not similarly related to the whole that is the cosmos. Any consciousness that might exist on an alternate physical substrate in AI systems is, therefore, artificial, or an artifact whose existence was made possible by the fact that natural evolution happened in our particular case to result in enough excess neuronal capacity to generate a symbolic universe.

Theoretical physicist Roger Penrose has made a similar

argument in *The Emperor's New Mind*. His position is essentially that AI computers can never be truly conscious because the laws of nature simply will not allow it.[18] Drawing on such diverse topics as fractal geometry, number theory, quantum physics, entropy, and cosmology, Penrose argues that the mind can reach insights that are in principle inacessible to AI computers. The basis for this conclusion is that all digital computers operate according to algorithms, or sets of rules prescribing how a problem is solved. Yet, as the mathematician Kurt Gödel demonstrated in his famous proof in the 1930s, there are problems that cannot be approached or solved with any system of algorithms. What Gödel proved in his theorem is that any mathematical system contains algorithmic propositions that cannot be proved within the mathematical system itself. In other words, in order to prove the validity of any mathematical theory one must go outside that theory and posit another mathematical proof. Yet since that proof cannot prove its own foundational propositions, we must go outside it to posit another proof, and so on ad infinitum.

After concluding that the human mind can lead us to truths that are not computable, Penrose suggests that consciousness and insight are governed by laws of physics that we have yet to discover. We are likely, speculates Penrose, to discover these unknown laws when Einstein's general theory of relativity, which deals with gravitational interactions and is mathematically incompatible with quantum theory, is quantized, or made mathematically consistent with quantum field theory. Penrose's hypothesis is that consciousness and insight are emergent properties of the neuronal organization of the brain that will eventually be explained in terms of quantum jumps from one energy state to another. Moreover, he also argues that a quantum theory of gravity will serve to explain why human consciousness perceives time, in contrast with the view of time implicit in the rest of quantum physics, as asymmetric, or as moving "forward" from past to future.

Assuming that quantum gravity provides this explanation, Penrose suggests that human consciousness will have to be viewed as intimately connected to the perceptible workings of nature throughout the history of the cosmos.

Another argument based on quantum physics, which is more extensively developed in a book that I coauthored with astrophysicist Menas Kafatos, takes a somewhat different approach to the matter-mind problem. The argument is that any form of consciousness that emerges on AI systems must be viewed as a simulation of human consciousness that cannot in principle be regarded as fully comparable to, or identical with, the actual dynamics of human consciousness.[19] The argument is premised on the assumption that the Copenhagen Interpretation of the epistemological situation in quantum physics, as it was articulated by Niels Bohr, is correct. Like Gödel's theorem, this interpretation allows one to assume that a mathematical description of the physical substrates of human consciousness, no matter how seemingly complete that description might be, cannot in principle be assumed to be utterly complete or exhaustive. This is so because mathematical theories cannot be assumed to have a real or prior existence outside of human subjective reality. In other words, quantum indeterminacy and wave-particle dualism obviate the prospect that all physical processes involved in human consciousness could be completely disclosed in mathematical theories.

Another related argument why this should in principle be the case involves an appeal to nonlocality as a fact of nature. Since all physical processes are on some level intimately connected with all other physical processes, a complete understanding of the physical substrates of human consciousness would necessarily require a simultaneous understanding of all events in the cosmos. Even without an appeal to the epistemological situation in quantum physics, there is obviously no way to achieve such an understanding. If one can accept these arguments, then a computer that passes the Turing test, no matter how dazzling its performance might be, would be nothing more than a simulation of human consciousness on a humanly engineered artifact. In other words, if the human brain is assumed to be intimately connected with the entire history of the cosmos, from its origins to the present, the reductionist scientific description of the parts associated with the physical substrate of consciousness cannot fully disclose the ultimate foundations of this consciousness.

Concluding Notes on the Evolution of Human Consciousness

Kierkegaard is known for his suggestion that a "leap of faith" must be made in the face of the apparent absurdity of human life to affirm belief in the existence of God. My sense of it is that we must make a similar leap to affirm the capacity of evolving human consciousness to discover the best means to survival, and to preserve and enhance the quality of human life on this planet. On a cosmic time scale, humankind is incredibly young to have come so far in understanding the conditions for its being and becoming in the cosmos. And it does seem likely that over time we will arrive at a more universal understanding of the value of human life and consciousness. Yet the dilemma here, of course, is that although our scientific world view may present us with alternate bases for understanding this value, it is perfectly silent when it comes to the actual business of valuation.

Modern theoretical physics does allow us to make the case that consciousness on the physical substrate of the human brain is intimately interconnected with the entire life of the cosmos, and that any form of consciousness that we engineer on an alternate physical substrate cannot be regarded as similarly interconnected. And it also seems obvious that Gödel's theorem, in conjunction with the new understanding of the character of scientific knowledge forced upon us by the quantum mechanical description of nature, clearly implies that a simulation of human consciousness based on a scientific understanding of the physical substrates of this consciousness is merely that— a simulation. Yet science per se says absolutely nothing about the status of human life and consciousness as a value, much less as an ultimate value.

The threat to the value of human life and consciousness in the technological era we are now entering is clearly not AI technologies per se—it is rather our seeming unwillingness to conceive of the proper uses of these technologies within the framework of an improved understanding of ourselves or, more specifically, of an improved understanding of the origins, nature, and character of human reality. Yet we are not likely to confront the arduous task of arriving at this improved understanding without a full commitment to preserving and protecting the ultimate value of human life and consciousness. If that commitment is to be made on a scale that makes a difference, it seems clear that more of us with active moral and philosophical imaginations must accept the challenge of becoming sufficiently expert in science and technology to enter into a meaningful dialogue with members of the culture of scientists-engineers. And it seems equally clear that scientists-engineers should strive to become sufficiently expert in the humanities and social sciences to realize that values have served a vital function in the evolutionary success of our species, and that values will be even more critical in the future than they have been in the past. For the members of the culture of scientists-engineers who fully appreciate the importance of values in this regard, the challenge is obviously to act on this understanding.

At the moment, however, all indications are that scientists-engineers and humanists–social scientists tend to operate as separate cultures, or in two rather isolated and distinct symbolic universes. If we are to avoid another massive tragedy in human affairs, this situation must change very rapidly. Perhaps the most appropriate way for members of either culture to realize the importance of their mutual cooperation with members of the other culture is to devote some time contemplating how utterly improbable it is, statistically or otherwise, that we should have come into existence as conscious beings.

Allow me to conclude by speaking more directly to readers who are members of the culture of scientists-engineers. Percy Bysshe Shelley's hyperbolic assertion in "A Defence of Poetry" that "Poets are the unacknowledged legislators of the World" was, for poets at least, new grounds for believing in their central role and importance in culture. Although it would also be hyperbolic to suggest that the planners and developers of new AI technologies have now assumed such an exalted role, there is an element of truth in this exaggeration. The planners and developers of these technologies will become increasingly empowered to legislate how various domains of human reality will be managed by the coming generations of AI computer systems and, therefore, to legislate the future of the world in these terms.

One of the attractions of the AI evolution-of-consciousness hypothesis is, of course, that it effectively frees planners and developers of new AI technologies from a sense of moral responsibility. If the future of AI technologies is predetermined by the lawful dynamics of evolution in a universe that is itself an information-processing system, how can one be morally responsible for doing what is inevitable? However effective this rationalization might be, it is, as I have attempted to demonstrate, merely a rationalization, and a terribly invidious one at that. It seems obvious that those who plan and develop new AI technologies must appreciate their central role and importance in human culture with the full and certain conviction that they are "free" moral agents. Although this is an awesome responsibility, decent men and women in the AI community will, I am convinced, accept it. And the rest of us should be quick to confer upon them the full measure of our admiration and respect.

Notes

Introduction

1. Hans Moravec, *Mind Children: The Future of Robot and Human Intelligence* (Cambridge, MA: Harvard University Press, 1988), 1.
2. Karel Capek, quoted in *Saturday Review*, July 1923.
3. Masahiro Mori, *The Buddha in the Robot: A Robot Engineer's Thoughts on Science and Religion*, trans. Charles S. Terry (Tokyo: Kosei, 1974), 178–80.

Chapter 1
Mind, Machines, and the Evolution of
Human Consciousness

1. John Kemeny, quoted in Arthur C. Clarke, *July 20, 2019* (New York: Macmillan Publishing Company, 1986), 70.
2. Marvin Minsky, quoted in Robert Jastrow, *The Enchanted Loom* (New York: Simon and Schuster, 1981), 165.
3. Claude Shannon, "Interview," *Omni*, August 1987, 65.
4. Robert Jastrow, *The Enchanted Loom*, 162.
5. See Michael Schrage, " 'Artificial Lifers' Are Relying on Software and Silicon to Emulate Evolution," *Washington Post*, 9 February 1990.
6. Jastrow, *The Enchanted Loom*, 86.

7. Hans Moravec, *Mind Children: The Future of Robot and Human Intelligence* (Cambridge, MA: Harvard University Press, 1988), 69.
8. James Anderson, quoted in William F. Allmann, "Designing Computers That Think the Way We Do," *Technology Review*, May–June 1987.
9. Jacob Bronowski, *The Identity of Man* (Garden City, NY: Natural History Press, 1965), 243.
10. See L. J. Siever, "Biological Markers in Schizotypal Personality Disorder," *Schizophrenia Bulletin* 11 (1985): 563–75.
11. Edward Beck, quoted in Richard M. Restak, *The Brain* (New York: Warner Books, 1980), 284.
12. Candace Pert, quoted in Judith Hooper and Dick Teresi, *The 3-Pound Universe* (New York: Dell, 1986), 71.
13. Joseph Weizenbaum, quoted in Grant Fjermedal, *The Tomorrow Makers* (New York: Macmillan Publishing Company, 1987), 140.

Chapter 2
The Mind Is Its Own Place:
The Human Brain as Reality Processor

1. See David Peat, *Artificial Intelligence: How Machines Think* (New York: Baen Book, 1985), 25–43.
2. Sir Charles Sherrington, *The Integrative Action of the Nervous System* (Cambridge: Cambridge University Press, 1947), 12.
3. Paul MacLean, "The Triune Brain, Emotion and Scientific Basis," in *The Neurosciences: Second Study Program*, ed. F. O. Schmitt (New York: Rockefeller University Press, 1970), 336–49.
4. Paul MacLean, quoted in Richard Restak, *The Brain*, (New York: Warner Books, 1970), 52.
5. Candace Pert, quoted in Judith Hooper and Dick Teresi, *The 3-Pound Universe* (New York: Dell, 1986), 42.

6. William Penfield and Herbert Jasper, *Epilepsy and the Functional Anatomy of the Human Brain* (Boston: Little, Brown, 1954), 60.
7. See Hooper and Teresi, *The 3-Pound Universe*, 68–104.
8. See Elizabeth F. Loftus and Geoffrey R. Loftus, "On the Permanence of Stored Information in the Human Brain," *American Psychologist* 35 (May 1980):409–20.
9. Roger Sperry quoted in Restak, *The Brain*, 196–97.
10. Michael S. Gazzaniga, *The Social Brain* (New York: Basic Books, 1980), 4.
11. Ibid., 28.
12. Ibid., 117.
13. James Watson, quoted in Hooper and Teresi, *The 3-Pound Universe*, 11.
14. See Heinz R. Pagels, *The Dreams of Reason* (New York: Simon and Schuster, 1988), 71–87.
15. See Alan Garfinkle, "A Mathematics for Physiology," *American Journal of Physiology* 245 (1983): R455–66.
16. See Roy Alan King, Jaschom D. Raese, and J. D. Barchas, "Catastrophe Theory of Dopaminergic Transmission: A Revised Hypothesis of Schizoprenia," *Journal of Theoretical Biology* 92 (1981): 273–400.
17. Cited in Hooper and Teresi, *The 3-Pound Universe*, 371.
18. See Arnold Mandell, "Statistical Stability in Random Brain Processes: Possible Implications for Polydrug Abuse in the Borderline Syndrome," in *Advances in Substance Abuse: Behavioral and Biological Research*, vol. 2, ed. Nancy K. Mello (Greenwich, CT: JAI Press, 1980).
19. Michael Arbib, *In Search of the Person* (Amherst, MA.: University of Massachusetts Press, 1985), 124.

Chapter 3
The Minds We Make:
The Present Generation of Computers

1. Hans Moravec, quoted in Arthur C. Clarke, *July 20,*

2019 (New York: Macmillan Publishing Company, 1986), 68.

2. Ibid., 69.

3. Azriel Rosenfeld, et al., "Report of the Research Briefing Panel on Computer Vision and Recognition," *Research Briefings* 1985 (Washington, D.C.: 1986), 94.

4. Berthold K. P. Horn and Katsuhi Ikeuchi, "The Mechanical Manipulation of Randomly Oriented Parts," *Scientific American*, August 1985, 100–111.

5. Tomasso Paggio, Vincent Torre, and Christof Koch, "Computational Vision and Regularization Theory," forthcoming in *Nature*.

6. Han Moravec, "Robots That Rove," quoted in Grant Fjermedal, *The Tomorrow Makers* (New York: Macmillan Publishing Company, 1987), 30.

7. Marvin Minsky, "Jokes and the Logic of Cognitive Unconscious," *MIT Memo No. 603*, November 1980.

8. Marvin Minsky, "The Intelligence Transplant," *Discover* 10, no. 10 (October 1989): 58.

9. See "General Computer Takes Charge," *New Scientist*, 21 April 1983, 153.

10. See "Crisis Management Under Strain," *Science* (31 August 1984): 907–9.

11. William F. Renfro, "Future Histories: A New Approach to Scenarios," *The Futurist*, March–April 1987, 38–41.

12. William F. Allman, "Designing Computers That Think the Way We Do," *Technology Review*, May–June 1987, 63.

13. See Minsky, "The Intelligence Transplant," 52.

14. See Sherry Turkle, *The Second Self* (New York: Simon and Schuster, 1984), 38–40.

15. See Michael Dertouzos, "The Multiprocessor Revolution," *Technology Review*, February–March 1986, 49–51.

16. Jospeph Wiezenbaum, "On the Impact of the Modern Computer," in *The Conscious Reader*, ed. Caroline Shrodes, et al. (New York: Macmillan Publishing Company, 1985), 469.

Chapter 4
The Neural-Network Revolution:
Modeling the Emergent Mind

1. John Hopfield, quoted in William F. Allman, *Apprentices of Wonder: Reinventing the Mind* (New York: Bantam Books, 1989), 91. This is a superb account of the neural-network revolution, and I am much indebted to it in this chapter.
2. Ibid., 14.
3. See Allman, *Apprentices of Wonder*, 90–91.
4. John Hopfield, quoted in William F. Allman, "Designing Computers That Think the Way We Do," *Technology Review*, May–June 1987, 63.
5. See Allman, *Apprentices of Wonder*, 95–97.
6. Ibid.
7. See James A. Anderson, "Cognitive and Psychological Computation with Neural Networks," *IEEE Transactions on Systems, Mind and Cybernetics*, SMC-13, no. 5 (September–October 1983).
8. See Gary Lynch, et al., "Cortical Encoding of Memory: Hypothesis Derived from Analysis and Simulation of Physiological Learning Rules in Anatomical Structures," in *Neural Connections and Mental Computations* (Cambridge, MA: MIT Press, 1987).
9. See Gerald Edelman, *Neural Darwinism* (New York: Basic Books, 1987).
10. See Marvin Minsky and S. Papert, *Perceptions* (Cambridge, MA: MIT Press, 1969).
11. See Minsky, *The Society of Mind* (New York: Simon and Schuster, 1986).
12. See T. J. Seynowski, P. K. Kiener, and G. E. Hinton, "Learning Symmetry Groups with Hidden Units: Beyond the Perceptron," *Physica*, 22D (1986): 260–75.
13. See Allman, *Apprentices of Wonder*, 163–65.
14. See Andre G. Barto and Richard S. Sutton, "Landmark Learning: An Illustration of Associative Speech," *Biological Cybernetics* 41 (1981): 1–8.
15. John R. Skoyles, "Training the Brain Using Neural Network Models," *Nature* 333 (2 June 1988): 401.

16. See Allman, *Apprentices of Wonder*, 135–36.
17. See Edward A. Feigenbaum and Pamela McCorduck, *The Fifth Generation* (Reading, MA: Addison-Wesley, 1983).
18. Cited in Allman, *Apprentices of Wonder*, 175.

Chapter 5
The Birth of the Mindlike Computer

1. Edward A. Feigenbaum and Pamela McCorduck, *The Fifth Generation* (Reading, MA: Addison-Wesley, 1983), 7–8.
2. Stephen G. Davis, "Superconductive Computer in Your Future," *Datamation*, 15 August 1987, 74–78.
3. Yasser S. Abu-Mostafa and Demetri Psaltis, "Optical Neural Computers," *Scientific American*, March 1987.
4. Eric Drexler, *Proceedings of the National Academy of Sciences*, 1986.
5. Material on Drexler is derived largely from interviews with Grant Fjermedal and published in *The Tomorrow Makers* (New York: Macmillan Publishing Company, 1987), 175–81.
6. Taizo Nishikawa, quoted in *Business Week*, 23 October, 1989, 112.
7. Marvin Minsky, quoted in Fjermedal, *The Tomorrow Makers*, 24.
8. Hans Moravec, *Mind Children: The Future of Robot and Human Intelligence* (Cambridge, MA: Harvard University Press, 1988), 37.

Chapter 6
The Ultimate Man-Machine Interface:
Who Shall Make the Journey to the Stars?

1. Hans Moravec, "Robots That Rove," quoted in Grant Fjermedal, *The Tomorrow Makers* (New York: Macmillan Publishing Company, 1987), 254–56.
2. Ibid., 139–40.

3. Joseph Weizenbaum, *Computer Power and Human Reason: From Judgment to Calculation* (San Francisco: W. H. Freedman, 1979), 241.
4. Ibid.
5. Claude Shannon, "Interview With Claude Shannon," *Omni* 87, no. 11 (August 1987): 64.
6. Nils Nilsson, quoted in David Ritchie, *The Binary Brain* (Boston: Little, Brown and Company, 1984), 179.
7. Moravec, *Mind Children: The Future of Robot and Human Intelligence* (Cambridge, MA: Harvard University Press, 1988), 158.
8. Ibid., 4.
9. Ibid., 121.
10. Ibid., 75.
11. Ibid., 128.
12. Ibid., 12.
13. Ibid., 17.
14. Ibid., 100.
15. Ibid., 137.
16. Herbert Dreyfus, *What Machines Can't Do: A Critique of Artificial Intelligence* (New York: Harper and Row, 1986); John Searle, *Minds, Brain and Science* (Cambridge, MA: Harvard University Press, 1984).
17. Karl R. Popper and John C. Eccles, *The Self and Its Brain*, parts I and II (Berlin: Springer-Verlag International, 1977).
18. See John Searle, "Minds and Brains Without Programs," in *Mindwaves: Thoughts on Intelligence, Identity and Consciousness*, ed. Colin Blakemore and Susan Greenfield (New York: Basil Blackwell, 1987), 210–23.
19. A. Newell and H. A. Simon, *Human Problem Solving* (Englewood Cliffs, NJ: Prentice-Hall, 1972).
20. Sherry Turkle, *The Second Self* (New York: Simon and Schuster, 1987), 312.
21. Carl Hewitt, quoted in Fjermedal, *The Tomorrow Makers*, 143.
22. Ibid., 143–44.
23. Ibid., 145.

Chapter 7
Fundamentals of Biological Computing:
A New Basis for Valuation

1. Charles J. Lumsden and Edward O. Wilson, *Promethian Fire* (Cambridge, MA: Harvard University Press, 1983), 42.
2. See Stephen Jay Gould, *Ontogeny and Phylogeny* (Cambridge, MA: Harvard University Press, 1977).
3. Vernon B. Mountcastle, "The View From Within: Pathways to the Study of Perception," *Johns Hopkins Medical Journal* 136 (1975): 109-31.
4. See Sue Taylor Parker and Kathleen Rita Gibson, "A Developmental Model for the Evolution of Language and Intelligence in Early Hominids," *Behavioral and Brain Sciences* 2, no. 3 (1979).
5. Philip Tobias, quoted in Seymour W. Itzkoff, *The Form of Man* (Ashfield, MA: 1983), 212.
6. See Alan Walker and Richard E. F. Leaky, "The Hominids of East Turkana," *Scientific American*, August 1978, 54-56; Donald Johanson and T. D. White, "A Systematic Assessment of Early African Hominids," *Science* 203 (1970): 321-30; and John E. Cronin, et al., "Tempo and Mode of Hominid Evolution," *Nature* 291 (March 1981): 113-22.
7. See Parker and Gibson, "Evolution of Language and Intelligence in Early Hominids," 367-408.
8. Clifford Geertz, quoted in Ruben Abel, *Man Is the Measure* (New York: Macmillian Publishing Company, 1976), 154.
9. Ludwig Wittgenstein quoted in Abel, 155. See also Ludwig Wittgenstein, *Philosophical Investigations* (New York: Macmillan Publishing Company, 1955.)
10. Ruth Benedict, quoted in Abel, 154.
11. Peter L. Berger and Thomas Luckman, *The Social Construction of Reality* (New York: Anchor Books, 1967), 23.

12. See Peter Drucker, *Landmarks for Tomorrow* (New York: Harper and Row, 1959).
13. See Dick Hanson, *The New Alchemists* (New York: Avon, 1982).
14. Garrett Hardin, *Nature and Man's Fate* (New York: Mentor Books, 1959), 56.
15. Stanley Edgar Hyman, *The Tangled Web: Darwin, Frazer and Freud as Imaginative Writers* (New York: Atheneum Books, 1962), 28–29.
16. Stephen Jay Gould, *The Panda's Thumb* (New York: Norton, 1982), 90–91.
17. Ibid., 92.
18. Ibid.
19. See Michael Schrage, " 'Artificial Lifers' Are Relying on Software and Silicon to Emulate Evolution," *Washington Post*, 9 February 1990.

Chapter 8
Paradigms, Paradoxes, and the Technological Future

1. Ivor Leclerc, "The Relation Between Science and Metaphysics," in *The World View of Contemporary Physics*, ed. Richard E. Kitchener (Albany, NY: S.U.N.Y. Press, 1988), 27.
2. Alexander Koyré, *Metaphysics and Measurement* (Cambridge, MA: Harvard University Press), 42.
3. Henry P. Stapp, "Spacetime and Future Quantum Theory," forthcoming in *Foundations of Physics*.
4. Albert Einstein, cited in Melic Capek, *The Philosophical Impacts of Contemporary Physics* (Princeton: Princeton University Press, 1961), 53.
5. Max Planck, *Where Is Science Going?* (London: G. Allen and Unwins, 1933), 24.
6. Albert Einstein, "Autobiographical Notes," in *Albert Einstein: Philosopher-Scientist*, ed. P. A. Schlipp (La Salle, IL: Open Court, 1969), 45.

7. Albert Einstein, quoted in *New York Post*, 28 November 1972.

8. Henry P. Stapp, "Quantum Theory and the Physicist's Conception of Nature: Philosophical Implications of Bell's Theorem," in *The World View of Contemporary Physics*, 38.

9. Richard Feynmann, *The Character of Physical Law* (Cambridge, MA: MIT Press, 1967), 130.

10. See Niels Bohr, *Atomic Theory and the Description of Nature* (Cambridge: Cambridge University Press, 1961), 4, 24; *Atomic Physics and Human Knowledge* (New York: John Wiley and Sons, 1958), 5, 8, 53, 94; and "Causality and Complementarity," *Philosophy of Science* 4, 293–94.

11. Stapp, "Quantum Theory and the Physicist's Conception of Nature," 54.

12. A. Aspect, J. Dalibard, and G. Roger, *Physical Review Letters* 49 (1982): 1804.

13. John S. Bell, *Physics* I (1964): 195.

14. Bernard d'Espagnet, *In Search of Reality* (New York: Springer-Verlag, 1981), 43–48.

15. Errol E. Harris, "Contemporary Physics and Dialectical Holism," in *The World View of Contemporary Physics*, 161.

16. Ibid.

17. Ibid., 162.

18. Roger Penrose, *The Emperor's New Mind* (New York: Oxford University Press, 1989).

19. Menas Kafatos and Robert Nadeau, *The Conscious Universe: Part and Whole in Modern Physical Theory* (New York: Springer-Verlag, 1990).

Index